Foundation
Geography in Action

Miranda Ashwell

Series Consultant: **Andy Owen**

Heinemann Educational Publishers
Halley Court, Jordan Hill, Oxford OX2 8EJ
A Division of Reed Educational & Professional Publishing Ltd

OXFORD MELBOURNE AUCKLAND
JOHANNESBURG BLANTYRE GABORONE
IBADAN PORTSMOUTH (NH) USA CHICAGO

First published 1996

99 98
10 9 8 7 6 5 4 3 2

ISBN 0 435 35066 8

Designed and produced by Gecko Ltd, Bicester, Oxon

Cover photos by Martin Colston

Printed in Spain by Mateu Cromo Artes Graficas SA

Acknowledgements

The authors and publishers would like to thank the following for permission to use photographs/copyright material (the numbers refer to the pages on which material appears):

ActionAid, *Common Cause*: extracts 7, 77; BBC *Wildlife*: extract, 71; ECO, Journal of the Environmental Information – Belize: extract, 76; CPA Family Polling Studies Centre: table, 16; bar chart (source Eurostat) 15; *The Daily Telegraph*: extract reproduced by permission of Ewan McNaughton Associates, 45; *The Economist*/Petrobras: advertisement, 87; Edward Arnold Publishers Ltd: M.Witherick and M.Carr, *The Changing Face of Japan*, map, 46, diagram, 49; Escritt, E. A: map, 81; *Financial Times*: graphs 24.2.94, 32 (source Barings), 2.11.92/1.3.95, 46, 1.3.95, 70, table 17.11.94, 47, extract 13.3.92, 89; Geographical Association: *Teaching Geography*, Momsen, graph, 83; table, 84; *The Guardian*: diagram, 25, extracts 32, 37, 92; *Guardian* Education: extract, 84, data for table 85; HarperCollins: Andrew Reed, *Issues in Development: Brazil*, Unwin Hyman, map, 88; HMSO, © Crown copyright is reproduced with the permission of the Controller of HMSO, map, 24, from *Global Climate Change* 2nd Edition table, 52, map, 53; *Hong Kong Year Book*: graph, 36; *The Independent on Sunday*: extract, 13, 73, graph, 49; *The Independent*: extracts by T McCarthy-Manila, 20, diagram, 44, map, 54, extract, 54; Longman: Knapp, Ross & McCare, *Challenge of the Human Environment*, pie chart, 9; Michelin: map, 63; National Power plc: data for table, 56; *New Internationalist: Geographical Studies of Development* 12/79, diagram, 17; *New Scientist*: map, 25; Ordnance Survey: Reproduced from the Ordnance Survey mapping with the permission of The Controller of HMSO © Crown Copyright, map, 78; Philip Allan Publishers: *Geography Review*, map, 64, diagram, 58, graph, 74; School of Geography and Earth Resources: *Geography*, map, 16; Shobunsha Co. Ltd, Tokyo: map, 41; Shropshire Star Newspapers Ltd: extract, 45; *From Area Resource Pack Brazil*, Steve Scoble, publ. by Stanley Thornes (Publishers) Ltd, Cheltenham. © Stanley Thornes (Publishers) Ltd: table, 86, map, 89; © Times Newspapers Limited 30.06.91: map '*Danger area: The Fens are now under serious threat from flooding*' by Gunter Greatwood *Sunday Times Magazine*, 53; Thompson Tour Operations Ltd: extract, graph, 73; UNEP: *World Atlas of Desertification*, 67; World Bank Atlas: map, 14; Warmer Bulletin, World Resource Foundation: extract, 42.

Photographs

ActionAid: 6/Liba Taylor, 7T/Morris Keyonzo, 7B/Jenny Matthews, 17/K. Ponnappa Subbaiah, 77B/Adam Hinton; Associated Press/Topham Picture Library: 10 & 20T, 25/G. Ramesh, 57; Peter Capener: 60 all; Christian Aid Photo Library: 91/E. Berrios; Coral Cay Conservation Ltd: 79 both; Gertrud and Helmut Denzau: 71; Environmental Picture Library: 42/Steve Morgan, 54T/Bob Edward, 54B/Roger Grace, 55/Paul Glendell; Friends of the Earth: 61R; Peter Furley: 74, 75, 78; Robert Harding Picture Library: 9 & 12/J. H. C. Wilson, 14L/Sassoon, 14R/James Strachan, 26/Gavin Hellier, 32/David Lomax, 40, 48/Elly Beintema, 64, 83L/C Bowman; The Hutchison Library: 30/R. Ian Lloyd, 31, 46/Michael MacIntyre; Peter Jackson: 80; David Job: 58; Frank Lane Picture Agency: 23/S. Jonasson, 66/David Hosking, 76B/Terry Whittaker; Magnum Photos: 36T/Patrick Zachmann, 36B & 69/Ian Berry, 84/Bruno Barbey; Janet Momsen: 35; David Munro: 76T, 77T; Mark Newham/Eye Ubiquitous: 62; NHPA: 90/Jany Sauvanet/E. Janes, 92T/Gerard Lacz; Andy Owen: 59; Panos Pictures: 33/Chris Stowers, 70/Roderick Johnson, 83R/Sean Sprague; Popperfoto: 18, 44R/Reuter; Carlos Reyes/Andes Press Agency: 85; Science Photo Library/NASA: 20B, 34, 61L; Spectrum Colour Library: 38/Raga; Frank Spooner Pictures: 92B/J. L. Bulcao; Still Pictures: 67/Mark Edwards, 93/John Maier; Thomson Worldwide, 1993: 73 both; Topham Picture Library: 27; Cynthia Widden: 44L.

How to use this book

Location globe
The country you are studying is shown on a map of the world.

Unit aims
The main ideas are found at the start of each unit.

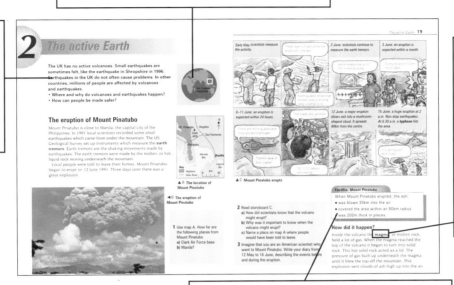

Keywords
Important words are printed in **bold**. These words are explained in the Glossary at the back of the book.

Factfile
Extra facts are given here.

Captions
All the pictures, graphs, maps, and newspaper articles have a caption. The letter next to the ▶ helps you to find the right source when you answer the questions.

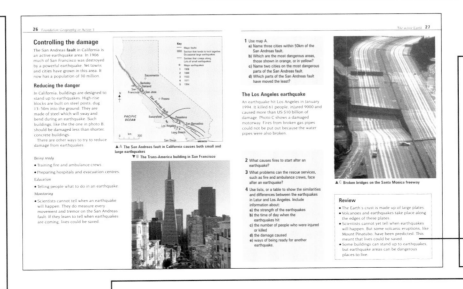

Review
This reminds you about the key ideas. It helps to read the review before you move on.

Index
This lists the topics, places, and ideas covered in the book. It gives the page numbers where they are described.

Contents

Population

In this unit we will look at the following questions:
- **why do people in some countries have many children?**
- **why is birth control important?**
- **what happens when people live longer?**

Youthful populations

Women in developing countries have more children than women in developed countries. Developing countries such as India have a **youthful population**. This means there is a large proportion of children in the population. Graph A compares the population of India with a developed country, the UK.

Children who work

About 44 million children work in India. Most work in factories and farms, but others do **informal work** like rag-picking. Over 100 000 children in Bangalore and Bombay are rag-pickers. They search the rubbish dumps to find anything that they can sell or recycle. This is dirty and dangerous work but it helps to keep the streets clean and save resources. Rag-pickers need 20 rupees (40 pence) a day to live on. This means that every day they must collect a pile of rubbish one metre high.

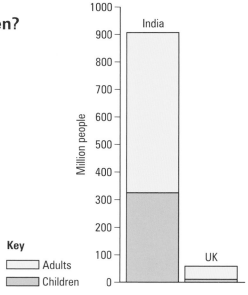

Million people (y-axis, 0 to 1000)

▲ A The population of India and the UK

Use graph A.
1 What is the population of:
  a) India
  b) the UK?

2 How many children live in India?

3 Which country has the greater proportion of children?

> I'm Sampangi. I'm 17 and I live in Bangalore, India. I've no parents. I used to be homeless. I moved from place to place, rag-picking to earn enough money to live. Sometimes the cops chased me, or older boys stole my things. Now I live in a hostel for street boys.

► **B Sampangi, a rag-picker**

Children support their families

◀ C Naiga looks after her baby sister. Local boys see that she is alone so they bully her

The two sisters in photo C live in Uganda. Naiga is only fourteen. When her parents died of AIDS she had to leave school. She had to look after her three younger brothers and sisters. In Naiga's village one out of every seven adults has AIDS. In July 1993, there were at least 100 000 AIDS orphans in Uganda. About 1.5 million Ugandans have the HIV virus. Many mothers with the HIV virus will pass the illness to their children.

4 Make a list of Sampangi's problems, and a list of Naiga's problems. Which problems do both children have?

5 a) Discuss what might be done to help *either* Sampangi *or* Naiga.
   b) Discuss how Sampangi and Naiga help others.

6 a) What are the problems facing children in the UK?
   b) How are they similar or different from those of children in other parts of the world?

7 Design a poster to show people about the problems faced by children in the world.

Children at play

Christopher Luka, from Malawi, did not buy his truck. He took time and effort to make it himself. Wood is often hard to find in African countries. So children all over Africa make toys from old tins, bottle tops, and bits of wire.

▲ D Adapted from *Common Cause*, January 1994

Children of the world

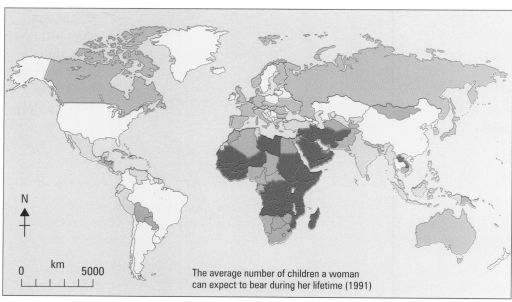

The average number of children a woman can expect to bear during her lifetime (1991)

◀ **A Family size changes from country to country**

Key

	6 children or more
	5 children or more
	4 children or more
	3 children or more
	2 children or more
	1 child

Why do women in developing countries have more children than women in developed parts of the world?

1 Use map A and an atlas. What is the average family size in the UK?

2 a) Use map A, diagram B, and an atlas to complete the following table.

	Average family size	GNP
Bangladesh		
Brazil		
Japan		

b) What link between wealth and average family size does your table show?

3 Use map A and an atlas. Would you expect Uganda to have a high or low GNP? Give reasons for your answer.

▼ **B The average wealth per person (or GNP) of three countries**

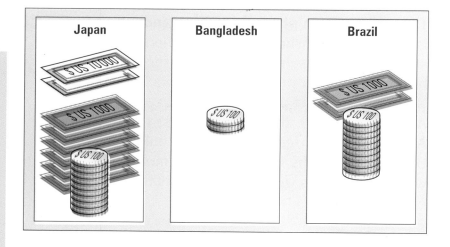

Japan	Bangladesh	Brazil

◀ **C The number of child deaths for every 1000 births**

Country	Infant mortality*	Family size
Afghanistan	162	6+
Bangladesh	108	
Nigeria	96	
Uganda	94	
India	88	
Kenya	64	
Brazil	57	
Mexico	36	
Argentina	29	
Spain	9	
UK	8	
Japan	5	

* **Infant mortality** means the number of children who die before they are one year old. These figures show the number of babies that die for every 1000 that are born.

THIMMAKKA — We farm two fields. We need our children to work on the land. How can I send them to school? They must work so that we can all eat.

PONNUTHI — That's unfair. Children must learn to read and write to have a good start in life.

MEERA — I agree. But I can't send my eldest daughter to school. I need her to help with my four younger ones. I'll only send the boys to school.

THIMMAKKA — Why should I waste money sending my daughter to school? She will soon get married and live with her husband's family.

PONNUTHI — That's wrong. Both boys and girls need to go to school. I have four girls. We borrow money and work hard to pay for their schooling.

INDIRA — You are all so lucky. My two children died before they were five. Now my husband and I have no help. Who will look after us when we are too old to work?

How do children help their families?

The Indian women in the photo show us ways in which children can help their families. Poor people in many developing countries choose to have many children. Children can go out to work. This brings in more money for the family. They also help with housework and farming. Poverty can lead to large families but having a large family does not make people poor. Diagram D shows that parents can have different reasons for having children.

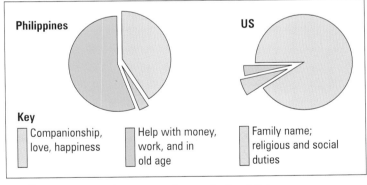

▲ **D** What parents want from their children

Key
- Companionship, love, happiness
- Help with money, work, and in old age
- Family name; religious and social duties

4 a) Copy table C. Fill in the table using map A and an atlas.
b) Your completed table will show a link between infant mortality and family size. Copy out the sentence below which explains that link correctly.

In countries with high numbers of child deaths the family size tends to be small.

In countries with low numbers of child deaths family sizes tend to be large.
In countries with high numbers of child deaths the average family size tends to be large.

5 List three reasons why the four Indian women would like to have large families.

6 Discuss how the life of a child in India might be different from your own life.

Birth rates

Most women in India have many children. This gives India a youthful population. India has a high **birth rate** or number of children born each year. Some parts of India have higher birth rates than others, as map A shows.

▲ A Birth rates in the different regions of India

◄ B A child wedding in Rajasthan

Child marriages

In some states people marry when they are very young and start having children sooner. Most girls in Rajasthan and Andhra Pradesh are married by the age of fifteen. Many children die in rural India so young girls can become widows. Widows are not allowed to remarry. Many of them run away to the city or become beggars.

1 Use map A.
a) Copy the following sentence choosing the right words.
In India the *southern/northern/central* states have the highest birth rates.
b) Which states have the lowest birth rates?

Asha, a young widow

Asha was married to a local boy when she was nine. She still lived with her parents in Rajasthan. At the age of fourteen she was about to join her husband and his family when he died. Asha became a widow. When she was fifteen she ran away from home. Now she is a maid in Delhi.

> When my husband died, my parents thought I brought bad luck. His family thought I was a witch! They treated me badly. I had to do all the housework. I could not go to weddings, or visit a new baby in case I passed on the bad luck. So, I ran away from home.

▲ C Asha's life changed when her husband died

Lowering the birth rate

Some states in India do not have high birth rates. Better health care and education in the state of Kerala has meant that the birth rate has fallen.

> In Kerala better health care has led to fewer child deaths. If children live to become adults, parents do not need to have so many children. People see that a small family is normal. Better education also helps to lower the birth rate. Women who go to university marry later and have fewer children.

▲ D Health worker in Kerala, south-west India

Average family size

Kerala	1.8
Uttar Pradesh	5.4
USA	2.1

Infant mortality (child deaths per 1000)

Kerala	17
India	85
USA	8

▲ E Family size and child deaths

2 Map A shows India's different birth rates. What colour would you expect on map A for:
 a) Rajasthan
 b) Kerala?
 c) Give reasons for your choices.

3 Do early marriages lead to women having larger or smaller families? Give reasons for your answer.

4 Discuss what might happen to widows like Asha if:
 a) they stay at home
 b) they run away from home.

5 Use pages 9–11 to make a list of reasons why people in India have large families.

Summary

People in developing countries have children for many reasons.
- Poor parents need children to earn money for the family.
- Children work on the family farm or business.
- Children look after their parents in old age.
- Where child deaths are common, parents have many children in case some of them die.
- An early marriage means more chance of having a large family.

Slowing down India's birth rate

The Indian government would like people to have smaller families. They are worried that the country will not be able to feed all of its people. There may not be enough houses for everyone.

Family planning means using birth control to plan the number of children in a family. It is an important issue for the Indian government as well as for ordinary people.

THIMMAKKA	*I don't want more children. But my husband won't use birth control. He wants another son to work on the farm.*
PONNUTHI	*Ask the health worker for help. He'll tell him about being sterilized.*
THIMMAKKA	*You're joking! He'd never do that.*
MEERA	*My husband says that sterilization makes men weak.*
INDIRA	*During the Emergency, men were forced into being sterilized. That happened to my uncle. Then they gave him a cheap radio!*
PONNUTHI	*What about other ways of birth control? I went to town last month and saw a shop that only sold condoms. I bought some too!*

MEERA	*I would be too afraid to do that. Anyway, I bet they cost too much.*
PONNUTHI	*Only half a rupee for three [about 1p].*
THIMMAKKA	*That's no good for me. I've never been to town in my life.*
INDIRA	*Why is it always women who worry about family planning? I got sterilized and then both my children died. Now I can't have any more.*

▲ **A Women's views on family planning**

India tries to slow down its birth rate

In 1975 the Indian government used emergency laws to force men to be sterilized. Today, the government encourages women to agree to sterilization. Schools are used as hospitals for a day or two to treat large numbers of women. The government gives 200 rupees (£4) to each sterilized woman. In 1993 about 4.1 million women were sterilized. Most of them were older women who already had children.

Is education the answer?

Next to a huge advert for condoms in a New Delhi street is a population clock. It counts the rate at which babies are born in India. It shows that a new baby is born every 1.5 seconds.

It is thought that the best contraception is education, not sterilization or condoms. One health worker said 'You could fill up a plane with condoms, fly over India and drop them out. But that won't help if the people below don't know what a condom is for.'

It seems that in states such as Kerala, where many people can read and write, families have fewer children. In other states where fewer people can read and write families are large.

But while India is wondering whether or not to educate its poor, the population continues to grow.

▲ **B** Adapted from *The Independent on Sunday*, 15 November 1992

	1950	1960	1970	1980	1990
Birth rate (per 1000 people)	44	42	38	35	31
Death rate (per 1000 people)	25	19	16	13	10

▲ **C** India's birth and death rates (1950–1990). The *death rate* is the number of people who die in a year

1 Use table C. Copy the sentences below, choosing the right words.
   a) India's birth rate *rose/fell* between 1950 and 1990.
   b) India's death rate *rose/fell* between 1950 and 1990.
   c) These changes mean India's population has *increased/decreased*.

2 Discuss India's attempts to control its birth rate. Use the following questions to help you.
   a) Why does India need to control its birth rate?
   b) What methods have been used?
   c) What problems are there in getting people to use family planning?
   d) How do you think the Indian government could best control the birth rate?

3 Use graph D. Copy and complete the table below.

	Average number of children	Females in secondary school
Japan		
Brazil		
India		
Ghana		

What pattern does your table show?

▼ **D** Family size and education

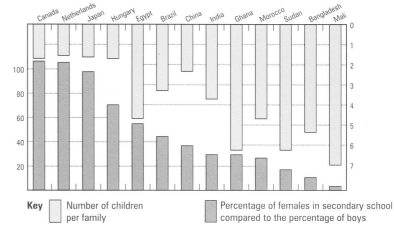

Key — Number of children per family — Percentage of females in secondary school compared to the percentage of boys

The world's ageing population

In most countries people now live longer than they did in the past. This is due to better health care. **Life expectancy** is the average age to which people can expect to live. As map A shows, life expectancy is higher in developed countries.

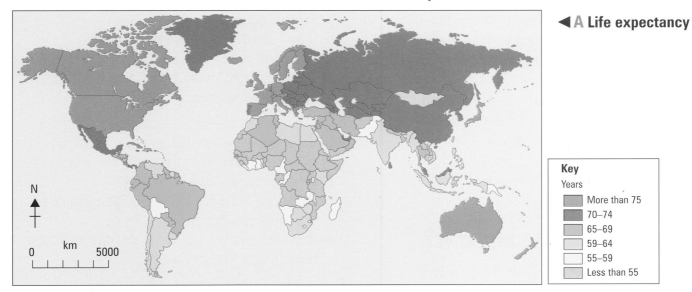

◀ **A Life expectancy**

Key

Years

	More than 75
	70–74
	65–69
	59–64
	55–59
	Less than 55

▼ **B D'igir Turoga is 58**

I have looked after camels and goats all my life. Young people who move into the town have forgotten the old ways. I can still find water underground. I knew how to find water before the scientists came with their equipment.

▼ **C Mama Ndoga is 70**

I'm still strong. At harvest time I carry sacks of pineapples back from the fields. I look after my grandchildren and great-grandchildren too.

▼ **D People now live longer**

Country	1950–55		1970–75		1990–95	
List 1	male	female	male	female	male	female
Afghanistan	31	32	38	38	43	44
Bangladesh	38	35	46	44	53	53
Brazil	49	53	58	62	64	69
Kenya	39	43	49	53	59	63
List 2						
Japan	62	66	71	76	76	82
Spain	62	66	70	76	74	80
UK	67	72	69	75	73	79
USA	66	72	68	75	73	80

1 Use map A. Find the average life expectancy in:
a) the UK   b) India   c) Kenya.

2 Use table D. Draw bar graphs to show changes in life expectancy in:
a) one country from list 1
b) one country from list 2.

3 Describe what your graph shows about life expectancy in the two countries.
a) How are they similar?
b) How are they different?

4 Read speech bubbles B and C. List ways in which older people can help:
a) their families   b) the community.

Europe's changing population

As people in Europe have become richer they have had fewer children. They no longer need children to earn money for the family. People are also living longer so the proportions of young and elderly people are changing. Graphs E and F show this.

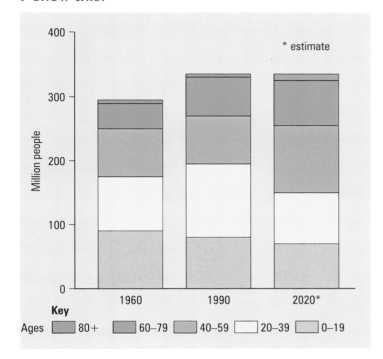

Key

Ages 80+ | 60–79 | 40–59 | 20–39 | 0–19

▲ **E How Europe's population is changing**

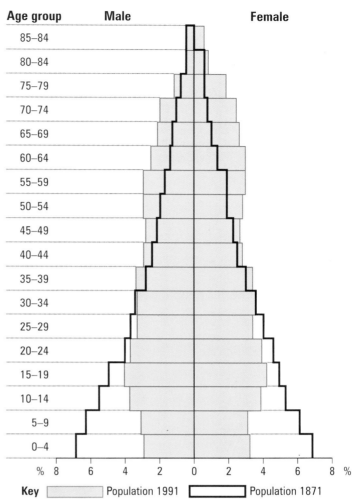

| Age group | Male | Female |

Key Population 1991 | Population 1871

▲ **F How the population of the UK has changed**

5 Use graph E. What is happening to the proportion of:
   a) children in Europe
   b) people over 60?

6 Use graph F. Copy the sentences below choosing the right words.
   a) The percentage of young children in the UK population has *increased/decreased*.
   b) The percentage of elderly people has *increased/decreased*.

7 Suggest reasons for the changes in the population of the UK and the rest of Europe.

8 People under 15 and over 65 who need support from others are called **dependants**. List the ways in which:
   a) you rely on adults
   b) people over 65 may rely on others.

9 Does D'igir Turoga rely on younger people? Discuss the ways in which elderly people can be independent.

Retirement in the UK

In the UK when people retire at the age of 60 or 65 they may have:
- a state **pension**, paid by the government
- a private pension, earned while they were working.

	Employment	Government pensions	Occupational/ private pensions	Savings	Other
Germany	21	34	34	11	-
Italy	1	46	49	2	2
Portugal	14	58	-	7	21
UK	8	50	25	17	-
Luxembourg	6	92	-	1	1

▲ **A Where income for people over 60 in Europe comes from (in percentages)**

▶ **B Percentage of retired people in the UK**

Key
Percentage of retired
- 13.5 – 15.5
- 12.5 – 13.4
- 12.0 – 12.4
- 11.5 – 11.9
- 11.0 – 11.4
- 9.0 – 10.9

No data

N

0   km   200

People who work pay taxes to the government.

Taxes are also used to pay pensions to retired people.

The government uses the money from taxes to run the country.

◀ **C How the government pays pensions**

1 Use map B and an atlas. Name a region in the UK with:
   a) the highest percentage of retired people
   b) the lowest percentage of retired people.

2 Governments in Europe are worried about the ageing population. Use diagram C to explain how:
   a) the amount of taxes being paid to the government will change
   b) the amount of pensions being paid by the government will change.

3 Use table A. Which country:
   a) gives most government help to pensioners
   b) gives least government help to pensioners
   c) will face the most difficulty in supporting an elderly population in the future?

4 Who should look after elderly people when they can no longer work? Discuss the parts played by:
   a) their children
   b) the state.

Review

- The population of many developing countries has a large percentage of young people. Poor families need their children to help with work.
- The birth rate is affected by many things, as diagram D shows.
- Better health care means that people live longer. In Europe, the population has almost stopped growing because people have small families. This means that there is a larger proportion of elderly people.

A better life for children in India

▲ **E** Sampangi

You read about Sampangi on page 6. He is not homeless now. He lives in a hostel run by a local charity. Here **street children** are given a home, meals, and an education. Local companies send their rubbish to the hostel so the children don't need to go onto the streets to collect it.

In Madras the city authorities pay hundreds of children to collect rubbish. They fill two bags, one with waste and one with things to recycle. They are paid a good wage of 800 rupees (£16) a month.

▼ **D** Things which affect the birth rate

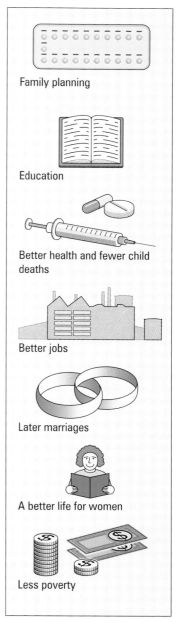

Family planning

Education

Better health and fewer child deaths

Better jobs

Later marriages

A better life for women

Less poverty

5 a) Use diagram D to list the things which help to lower the birth rate.
b) Which things do you think are the most important? Give reasons for your answer.

6 Write about the population of *either* the UK *or* India. Include information on:
a) family size
b) birth rates
c) life expectancy
d) birth control and population changes.

2 The active Earth

The UK has no active volcanoes. Small earthquakes are sometimes felt, like the earthquake in Shropshire in 1996. Earthquakes in the UK do not often cause problems. In other countries, millions of people are affected by volcanoes and earthquakes.
• Where and why do volcanoes and earthquakes happen?
• How can people be made safer?

The eruption of Mount Pinatubo

Mount Pinatubo is close to Manila, the capital city of the Philippines. In 1991 local scientists recorded some small earthquakes which came from under the mountain. The US Geological Survey set up instruments which measure the **earth tremors**. Earth tremors are the shaking movements made by earthquakes. The earth tremors were made by the molten, or hot, liquid rock moving underneath the mountain.

Local people were told to leave their homes. Mount Pinatubo began to erupt on 12 June 1991. Three days later there was a great explosion.

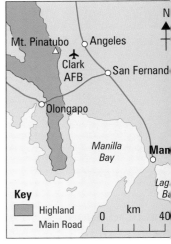

▲ **A** The location of Mount Pinatubo

◄ **B** The eruption of Mount Pinatubo

1 Use map A. How far are the following places from Mount Pinatubo
a) Clark Air Force base
b) Manila?

▲ C **Mount Pinatubo erupts**

2 Read storyboard C.
  a) How did scientists know that the volcano might erupt?
  b) Why was it important to know when the volcano might erupt?
  c) Name a place on map A where people would have been told to leave.

3 Imagine that you are an American scientist who went to Mount Pinatubo. Write your diary from 12 May to 16 June, describing the events before and during the eruption.

Factfile: Mount Pinatubo

When Mount Pinatubo erupted, the ash:
● was blown 30km into the air
● covered the area within an 80km radius
● was 200m thick in places.

How did it happen?

Inside the volcano the **magma**, or molten rock, held a lot of gas. When the magma reached the top of the volcano it began to turn into solid rock. This hot solid rock acted as a lid. The pressure of gas built up underneath the magma, until it blew the top off the mountain. This explosion sent clouds of ash high up into the air.

The effects of the eruption

▲ A People flee as ash and heavy rain fall

Thousands of people fled south as scientists warned that the volcano, Mount Pinatubo, was about to blow apart. Three towns and an air force base are in danger.

At midnight volcanic dust fell on Manila, covering buildings and cars. Ash also blocked Manila airport.

People began to panic. In Angeles City 100 people were trapped when the roof of a bus station was crushed by volcanic rock and ash. In Subic Bay people stayed indoors as rocks as large as tennis balls fell from the sky.

▲ B Adapted from *The Independent*, 16 June 1991

1 Use photo A and extract B.
  a) List the first effects of the eruption.
  b) List three ways in which the eruption endangered lives.
  c) Imagine that you are one of the people in photo A. Describe what it was like having to leave your home.

2 Use satellite photo C. How far was ash blown to the north-west of the crater?

► C Satellite photo of Pinatubo. The red colour is ash. The dark areas are rivers filled with mud. These mudflows swept into the valleys after heavy rain

0   km   10

Crater

N

Immediately after the eruption

- 200 000 buildings were destroyed by ash.
- Six people were killed.
- 250 000 people were made homeless.
- There was no power, or clean water.
- Ash covered the fields of 40 000 farmers.

Four months after the eruption

- There were 700 deaths from diseases caused by lack of clean water.
- People were starving.
- 200 000 people still could not return to their homes.
- 60 000 people had lost their jobs.

Long-lasting changes

Photo C shows the new crater and lake made when the volcano top blew off. Now any heavy rain turns the ash into mud. This causes mudflows which are like rivers of fast-flowing concrete. They cause damage and deaths.

The eruption affected the rest of the world. Ash from the volcano entered the atmosphere. This meant that less of the sun's energy could reach the Earth. World temperatures will be almost 1 °C lower than usual until the ash settles.

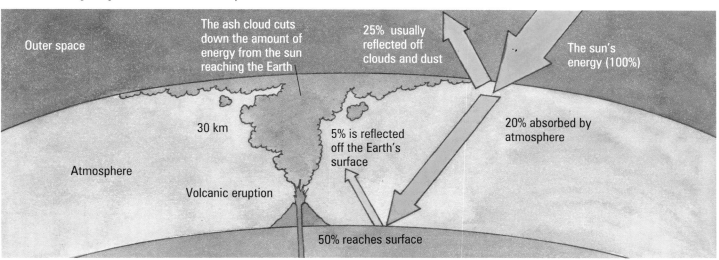

▲ **D** How the Pinatubo eruption affected the Earth's atmosphere. The arrows show how the sun's energy usually travels through the atmosphere. The Pinatubo eruption added extra dust to the atmosphere so more energy was reflected. This means that less energy reaches the Earth's surface. So world temperatures will be lower until the dust has gone

3 List the ways in which local people were affected by the eruption
  a) immediately after the eruption
  b) in the following months.

4 The environment was also affected by the eruption. Explain the effect of heavy rain on the volcanic ash.

5 Use the data below of rainfall in Manila. In which months would you expect most damage from mudflows? Give a reason for your answer.

Jan	Feb	Mar	Apr	May	Jun	Jul	Aug	Sep	Oct	Nov	Dec
23	13	18	33	130	254	432	422	356	193	145	66 (mm)

6 Explain in your own words or draw a diagram to show how the eruption affected the Earth's atmosphere.

Where are volcanoes found?

Map A shows many volcanoes around the rim of the Pacific Ocean. Many of these volcanoes, like Mount Pinatubo, have erupted with great force. Eruptions happen when magma, or molten rock, rises through the Earth's crust. In some places the Earth's solid crust is being destroyed in this way. The Pacific Rim is one of these places.

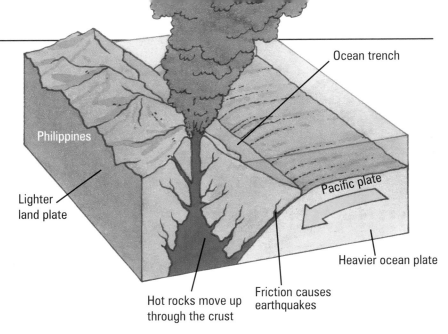

▲ **B** Along the Pacific Rim, plates in the Earth's crust move against each other. This causes earthquakes and volcanic eruptions

1 Use map A and an atlas.
  a) Name the countries where you will find the following volcanoes:
    (i) Cotopaxi   (ii) Krakatau   (iii) Fuji.

  b) Match each of these volcanoes with the right latitude and longitude references from this list:
    35N 139E   02S 79W   07S 105E.

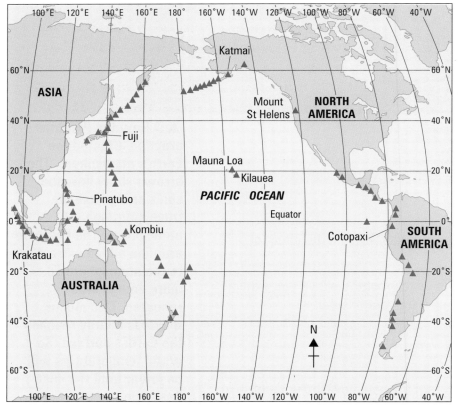

◄ **A** The volcanoes of the Pacific Rim. Volcanoes are found in places where the Earth's crust is being broken. The Earth's crust is split into *plates* which move and push against each other

Making new crusts

In other places the Earth's crust is moving apart. As the old crust is torn apart, magma rises to fill the gap and makes a new crust. The crust under the Atlantic Ocean is spreading in this way. A line of volcanic islands can be found where the new crust is being made. Iceland is the largest of these volcanic islands.

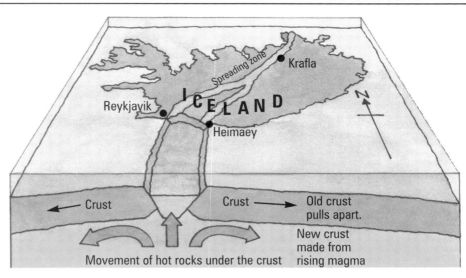

▲ C **How new crust is made in the Atlantic**

▲ D **A volcano erupts in Iceland.** *Lava*, **or molten rock, from a volcano erupts at over 1000 °C**

Using the Earth's heat

People use the heat from the volcanic rocks in Iceland. At Heimaey cold water is heated by underground rocks which are still hot from an eruption in 1973. This hot water is then pumped around buildings in the town to warm them. In Krafla the crust is spreading at the rate of 40cm a year. Here water is pumped 2000m into the crust. It returns as super-heated steam. This steam works turbines which make 38 megawatts of electricity. This is enough for 30 000 homes. Heat from rocks is called **geothermal energy**.

2 Match the two halves of these sentences.
  a) The Earth's crust is split into…
  b) Earthquakes and volcanoes on the Pacific Rim occur when…
  c) Volcanoes in Iceland occur when…
    (i)   …heavy ocean plates are destroyed under lighter plates.
    (ii) …plates with molten rock below.
    (iii) …the Earth's crust moves apart and magma rises to the surface.

3 Name one way in which the volcanic eruptions in Iceland and the Pacific Rim are different.

4 How do the Icelanders use the Earth's heat, or geothermal energy, in:
  a) Heimaey   **b)** Krafla?

The Earth's crust

The Earth's crust is made up of several large **plates**. These plates fit together like a jigsaw, as you can see in map A. Volcanic eruptions and earthquakes happen along the edges of the plates.

Plate movement

Movement of the plates causes volcanic eruptions and earthquakes. There are two types of movement.

● Continental plates crash into each other, and push upwards. Look at diagram A.

● Parts of one ocean plate sink below another. This can push up molten rock to make volcanoes. This is called **subduction**. Friction between the plates causes earthquakes.

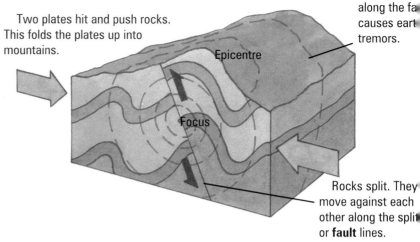

Two plates hit and push rocks. This folds the plates up into mountains.

Epicentre

Focus

Moveme[nt] along the fa[ult] causes eart[h] tremors.

Rocks split. They move against each other along the split or **fault** lines.

▲ **A How plates crashing into each other lead to earthquak[es]**

1 Copy the following sentences choosing the right words.
   a) The North American plate is moving *away from/towards* the European plate.
   b) The Nazca plate is *sliding under/moving away from* the South American plate.
   c) Earthquakes are most common where two plates are *moving apart/meeting*.

▼ **B The Earth's plates, showing the location of volcanoes and earthquakes**

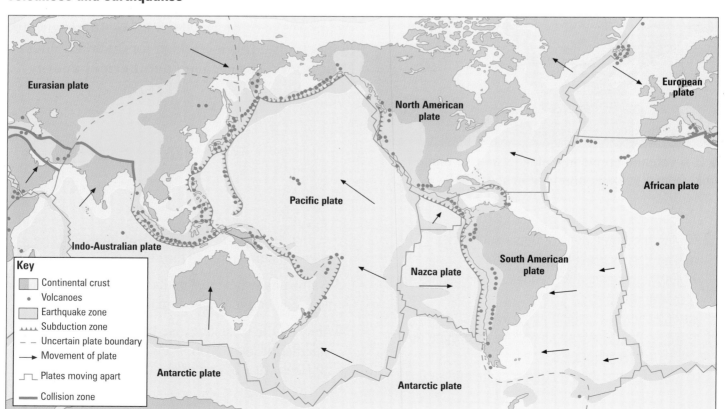

Eurasian plate

North American plate

European plate

African plate

Pacific plate

Indo-Australian plate

Nazca plate

South American plate

Antarctic plate

Antarctic plate

Key
- Continental crust
- • Volcanoes
- Earthquake zone
- Subduction zone
- – – Uncertain plate boundary
- → Movement of plate
- Plates moving apart
- Collision zone

Earthquake!

There was an earthquake in central India on 30 September 1993. The centre of an earthquake is known as the **epicentre**. Latur was close to the epicentre. Although the earthquake measured only 6.4 on the Richter Scale, it damaged over 80 villages. Clay and stone houses fell, killing 10 000 people.

These houses had thick earth walls and heavy beams to hold up the deep soil on the roofs. The walls had no cement to make them strong. They broke easily during the earthquake, which is why so many people were killed.

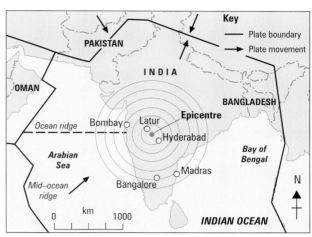

▲ C **Location of the Latur earthquake**

▲ D **Earthquake damage in Latur, India**

The local government is building 28 000 new homes. These houses need to be able to bend and sway. This means that they will be less likely to collapse in an earthquake.

First I heard a loud rumble, then a bang. The earth was rocking like a boat. Then I saw the tin roof of my house falling on top of me. I blacked out.

▶ E **An earthquake survivor**

2 Use map C. The Latur earthquake was felt in many parts of India. How far from the epicentre is:
a) Bombay   **b)** Bangalore?
3 Many people died in the Latur earthquake. Why were there so many deaths?
4 Why will the new houses shown in diagram F be safer in an earthquake?

▼ F **How the new houses could help save lives**

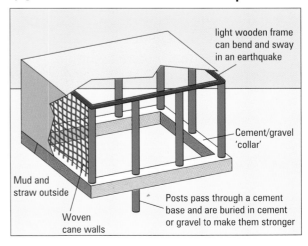

Controlling the damage

The San Andreas **fault** in California is an active earthquake area. In 1906 much of San Francisco was destroyed by a powerful earthquake. Yet towns and cities have grown in this area. It now has a population of 30 million.

Reducing the danger

In California, buildings are designed to stand up to earthquakes. High-rise blocks are built on steel posts, dug 13–50m into the ground. They are made of steel which will sway and bend during an earthquake. Such buildings, like the the one in photo B, should be damaged less than shorter, concrete buildings.

There are other ways to try to reduce damage from earthquakes.

Being ready

• Training fire and ambulance crews.

• Preparing hospitals and evacuation centres.

Education

• Telling people what to do in an earthquake.

Monitoring

• Scientists cannot tell when an earthquake will happen. They do measure every movement and tremor on the San Andreas fault. If they learn to tell when earthquakes are coming, lives could be saved.

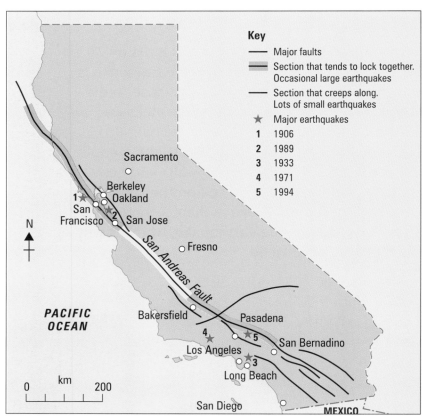

Key

— Major faults

▬ Section that tends to lock together. Occasional large earthquakes

— Section that creeps along. Lots of small earthquakes

★ Major earthquakes

1 1906
2 1989
3 1933
4 1971
5 1994

▲ **A The San Andreas fault in California causes both small and large earthquakes**

▼ **B The Trans-America building in San Francisco**

1 Use map A.
  a) Name three cities within 50km of the San Andreas fault.
  b) Which are the most dangerous areas, those shown in orange, or in yellow?
  c) Name two cities on the most dangerous parts of the San Andreas fault.
  d) Which parts of the San Andreas fault have moved the least?

The Los Angeles earthquake

An earthquake hit Los Angeles in January 1994. It killed 61 people, injured 9000 and caused more than US $10 billion of damage. Photo C shows a damaged motorway. Fires from broken gas pipes could not be put out because the water pipes were also broken.

2 What causes fires to start after an earthquake?

3 What problems can the rescue services, such as fire and ambulance crews, face after an earthquake?

4 Use lists, or a table to show the similarities and differences between the earthquakes in Latur and Los Angeles. Include information about:
  a) the strength of the earthquakes
  b) the time of day when the earthquakes hit
  c) the number of people who were injured or killed
  d) the damage caused
  e) ways of being ready for another earthquake.

▲ C **Broken bridges on the Santa Monica freeway**

Review

- The Earth's crust is made up of large plates.
- Volcanoes and earthquakes take place along the edges of these plates.
- Scientists cannot yet tell when earthquakes will happen. But some volcanic eruptions, like Mount Pinatubo, have been predicted. This meant that lives could be saved.
- Some buildings can stand up to earthquakes, but earthquake areas can be dangerous places to live.

3 Asian revolution

For several years now the economies of south-east Asia have been growing quickly. Yet the economies of European countries have hardly grown at all.

- How have some Asian countries grown so fast?
- How are some Asian countries improving their economies?

The tigers of Asia

South Korea, Taiwan, Hong Kong, and Singapore are sometimes called 'the tigers of Asia'. This is because their economies have become very strong in the past 30 years. Wealth has been created faster in these countries than in Europe or the USA. Other Asian countries such as Malaysia and China are also growing stronger, as map A shows.

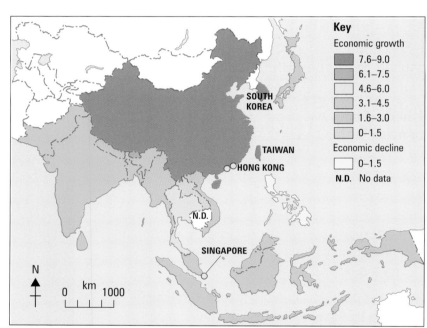

Key

Economic growth

■	7.6–9.0
■	6.1–7.5
□	4.6–6.0
■	3.1–4.5
■	1.6–3.0
□	0–1.5

Economic decline

□	0–1.5
N.D.	No data

▲ **A Economic growth in Asia 1980–1991**

1 Use an atlas and map A to name two countries with the same growth rate as:
  a) Taiwan **b)** Singapore
  c) with little or no economic growth.

Malaysia

Malaysia became independent from Britain in 1957. Its wealth came from exporting two raw materials, or **primary commodities**. These were rubber and tin. Prices paid for exported raw materials do not go up as quickly as the cost of imported manufactured goods. This means that countries whose wealth comes from exporting raw materials often become poorer year after year. Diagram B shows how this happens.

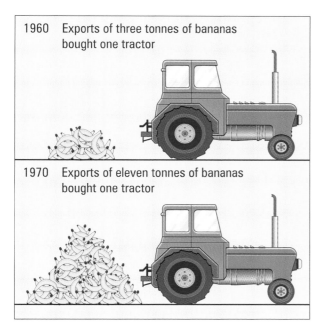

1960   Exports of three tonnes of bananas bought one tractor

1970   Exports of eleven tonnes of bananas bought one tractor

▲ **B** The price of raw materials (like bananas) does not rise as fast as the price of manufactured goods (like tractors)

▼ **C** Malaysia

New industries

Malaysia developed new industries, such as electronics, plastics, clothing, steel, and cement. Developing new and different industries is called **diversification**. Malaysian people could now buy goods made in Malaysia, so fewer goods had to be imported. Malaysia also earned more money by exporting these goods.

▼ **D** Rubber producing countries

Indonesia	1284
Malaysia	1250
Thailand	1200
India	330
China	280

(1000s of tonnes)

▼ **E** Percentage of Malaysia's export of primary commodities

	1960	1974	1990
Rubber %	74	30	9
Tin %	20	20	5

Tropical hardwoods are cut, mainly for sale in Japan.

Most industry is in the urban areas, particularly in Penang

Cities have a mix of Malays, Chinese, and Indians.

Most Malay people live in rural areas and grow rice.

2 Look at diagram B.
   a) Name the primary commodity.
   b) Name the manufactured goods.
   c) Which has risen most in price?
   d) Explain how this affects a country which relies on exporting primary commodities.

3 a) Name Malaysia's primary commodities.
   b) Use table E to draw up pie charts showing Malaysia's **exports** in 1960 and 1990. Your charts will each need three sections with the headings 'Rubber', 'Tin' and 'Other'.
   c) Describe the trend shown by your pie charts.

Malaysia's electronics industry

Malaysia is the world's third largest producer of **semiconductors** or microchips. Many Malaysian factories belong to foreign companies which are based in Japan, Singapore, the USA, or Europe. These firms are called **transnational companies (TNCs)**. Examples are Sharp, Sony, and Hitachi. In Malaysia they make electronic parts, disk drives, computers, TVs, and stereos. TNCs come to Malaysia because:

- taxes are low and there is a ten-year tax-free period
- wages are low – Malaysian software engineers earn five times less than in Germany
- Malaysia has no labour problems – workers do not strike or demand more pay.

The benefits of manufacturing

New factories have brought many new jobs, mostly for poor, rural Malay women. One million people now have jobs in manufacturing industries. Many new jobs are highly skilled. In 1985, thirteen US firms in Malaysia spent US $100 million training Malaysian engineers and technicians.
Workers look around for the best jobs. Firms find different ways to make people want to work for and stay with their company, as advert B shows.

▲ **A** Malay women working in the electronics industry

Jobs for women

Malay women from poor rural areas have also found jobs, but most of their work is semi-skilled. Some factory workers are paid only for the work they have done, not a fixed wage. This is called **piece-rate**. The women have to work quickly but carefully. They might be checking electronic parts or packing boxes.

Malaysia's problem is that it has a small population, so there are not enough people to work in the factories. The government wants people to have more children – not fewer as in other developing countries.

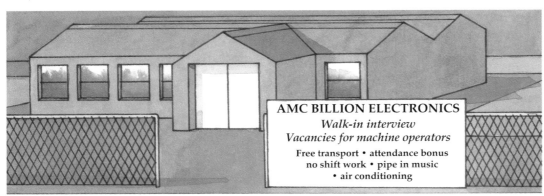

AMC BILLION ELECTRONICS
Walk-in interview
Vacancies for machine operators
Free transport • attendance bonus
no shift work • pipe in music
• air conditioning

◀ **B** There is a shortage of workers in Malaysia. Firms try to make their jobs sound attractive so that people will want to work for them

▲ C **A Malaysian village**

1 What is a TNC?

2 a) Why do TNCs open new factories in Malaysia?
  b) How have TNCs helped Malaysia?

3 a) What is 'piece-rate' work?
  b) Why do companies pay piece-rates?
  c) Do you think workers like piece-rate work? Why, or why not?
  d) What type of work is suitable for piece-rates?

4 How do factories help Muslim women come to work?

How has life changed for the Malay people?

Malaysia has a population of 18 million. It is made up of Chinese, Indian, and Malay people. Most people are Malay. It is the lives of young Malay women that have changed most. They have moved from the countryside to work in factories. Many Malays are Muslims. It goes against Muslim beliefs for girls to work outside the home. So firms work hard to take care of these women. Factory buses take them from their villages to Penang. Firms also provide hostels.

Jobs in manufacturing

The percentage of people working in manufacturing is growing. In the future jobs may be lost as more computers and robots are used in the factories. A factory in Penang, for example, makes 1.5 million rubber gloves a day using Malay rubber. New technology means the factory has only 54 workers.

▼ D

I used to work in the fields, growing rice and vegetables. But now, because of the factories, there is no one to look after the fields.

My mother used to do village work. It's better now that I send her money. Living in the hostel is fun. I go jogging and shopping with my friends.

5 Look at advert B. Make an advert for a job in a Penang factory. Your advert should:
  a) describe work conditions
  b) encourage Muslim women to apply.

Singapore and its people

Singapore is a small city state at the tip of the Malayan **peninsula**. You can see it on map A on page 28. It wants to become the wealthiest and most highly skilled country in Asia. Since the late 1960s its **economy** has grown three times faster than the UK economy. This success comes from exporting a wide range of goods, from electronics to medicines. Transnational companies (TNCs) make up 80% of manufacturing firms.

Average yearly incomes (GNP US$ – GNP or Gross National Product shows the wealth of a country)
▼ A

	Singapore	UK
1991	12 890	16 750
1992	15 750	17 760
1993	17 010	18 115
1994	18 370	18 839

▼ **B** Adapted from *The Guardian*, 12 December 1994

A future with computers

Singapore is looking forward to a future with computers. For example, schools could work out their budgets and timetables on computers. It would cost £9 million to set up. But it would save £6 million each year. Teachers would then have more time for other work. Children could do homework on a home computer, and send it into school by modem. A computer might even mark some of the homework!

The National Information Infrastructure plans to link every home to computers by the year 2005. Many new ideas will be possible using optical fibres. These can carry unlimited information. For example, patients at home could be linked to the hospital by a bedside computer. Electronic road signs could warn drivers about road conditions. Bus stops may show the time of the next bus.

▲ **C** An *aerial view* of Singapore

▼ **D** Manufacturing in Singapore

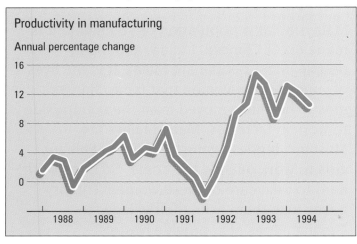

Productivity in manufacturing

Annual percentage change

1 Use table A. Copy the sentences below choosing the right words.

In 1991 incomes in Singapore were much *higher/lower* than incomes in the UK.
Incomes in both Singapore and the UK have been *rising/falling*. Incomes in Singapore are rising at a *slower/faster* rate than in the UK.

2 Use graph D.
   a) In which year was manufacturing in
   Singapore:
   (i) the lowest   (ii) the highest?
   b) Is manufacturing output in Singapore
   increasing or decreasing?

Population change

Singapore is very small. It covers an area of
42km by 23km. In the 1960s its
government was worried about over-
population. They encouraged couples to
have only two children. Parents who had
more than two children got little help with
housing or benefits. By the mid-1970s the
population had almost stopped growing.
   But in the 1980s the government needed
young, highly skilled people to work in
Singapore's industries. The government
now encourages well educated women to
have more children. Women with good
school results can have £3000 for each of
their three children. But poor, or less
educated, women are offered money to be
sterilized.

Workers from abroad

Singapore still does not have enough
workers of its own. More workers are
needed for low-skilled, low-paid jobs. 40%
of its workers come from other countries,
such as the Philippines and Malaysia.

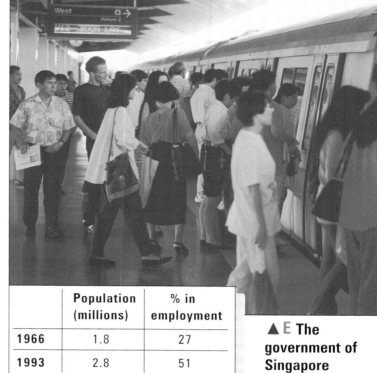

▲ **E** The
government of
Singapore
believes that
people are its
greatest resource

	Population (millions)	% in employment
1966	1.8	27
1993	2.8	51

▲ **F** Singapore's growing work force

3 Read extract B. List three new developments that
Singapore expects from information technology.

4 What was Singapore's population policy:
   a) from 1960 to 1980
   b) from the mid-1980s to now?

5 Discuss population policies in Singapore and India
(pages 12–13). Use these questions to help you.

   a) What worries did each country have about
   its population?
   b) How has each country's population policy
   changed?
   c) What are your opinions of these population
   policies? Are they fair?

China

China was cut off from the world until 1978. Chinese people could not travel, read, or hear about western countries. Since 1978 China has allowed contact with foreign countries. It wants to do business with the rest of the world. How has this affected China?

Guangdong province

In 1993 the economy of Guangdong grew by 25%. This makes it one of the fastest growing economic regions in the world. Foreign firms are attracted by low taxes in areas called Special Economic Zones. Firms from Hong Kong, Taiwan, Europe, and the USA set up factories in these areas. This has brought money into the province. Many Hong Kong firms are moving to Guangdong because they can pay lower wages. Average factory wages in Hong Kong are HK $266 (£22) a day. In China workers would be paid HK $25 (about £2.10).

---

1 Use map B and photo A.
  a) Match the grid references to the places:
Guangzhou	0323
Hong Kong Island	0329
Zhuhai	0722.

  b) Give grid references for:
  (i) Shenzhen   (ii) Macau.

▼ **A** Satellite photo of Guangdong

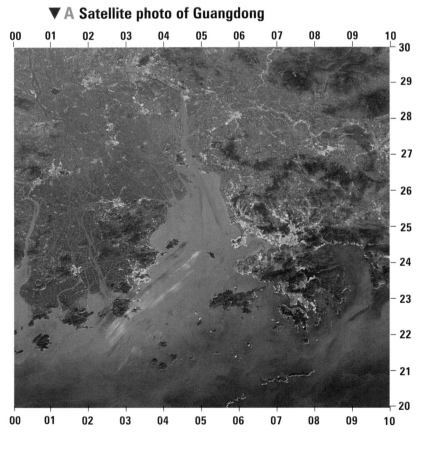

▼ **B** Guangdong Province

1986	1987	1988	1989	1990	1991	1992
2800	3700	5400	5600	6600	10 100	20 000

▲ C Money spent by foreign companies setting up businesses in China (US $ million)

Case study: the Haifong shoe factory

The Haifong shoe factory in Guangdong province employs 7000 people, mainly young women. They earn about £7.50 a week. The factory makes women's shoes for American supermarkets. It is owned by the Chinese army and a firm from Taiwan. This means that the Chinese can learn about manufacturing and exporting from the Taiwanese.

▲ D Chinese women working in a Guangdong factory

My firm moved here because wages are ten times lower than in Taiwan. Chinese girls learn quickly and work very hard. They know they are lucky to have work. So we can make better shoes here than we can in our Taiwanese factory.

I'm from Sichuan in central China. I like my factory work but the rules are very strict here. For example, we must not talk while we work. I live in the factory hostel. I save as much money as I can to send home to my family. Every year we are given the train fare to go home for a visit. One day I hope to live in my village again.

▲ E

2 a) How do joint projects like the Haifong shoe factory help China?
  b) How do they help foreign firms like the Taiwanese company?

3 Give two reasons why Hong Kong factories are moving to China.

4 a) Explain why Chinese girls want to work in factories.
  b) What might they find hard about factory work?

5 Use graph C.
  a) Draw a bar graph showing foreign investment in China.
  b) Describe the trend your graph shows.

▲ A The growth of industry in Shenzhen has made some people rich

▼ B Job changes in Hong Kong

The effects of fast growth

Migrants have moved to Guangdong province from all over China. How does this affect:
- the cities they move to
- the rural areas they leave?

Case study: Shenzhen

Before 1978 Guangdong was a farming area and Shenzhen was a small town. Now it is a busy city. Some Chinese people became rich very quickly. It is hoped that some of this new wealth might also reach the poor as more jobs are created. But too many people are moving to the city. At Chinese New Year over 100 000 people arrive each day. Some return home when they cannot find work, but others turn to crime or begging in order to live. Some become prostitutes.

Number of jobs			% job losses				0	% job gains				
1991	1993		40	30	20	10		10	20	30	40	50
132 900	146 400	Health									40+	
126 600	133 800	Ferries/airport								25		
375 200	452 200	Import/exports								20		
100 800	112 100	Banks							10			
139 100	140 900	Printing							2			
142 700	128 200	Plastics			30							
117 300	111 800	Computers			20							
187 500	134 800	Clothing			25							
198 700	175 700	Textiles			15							
205 500	198 200	Retailing				5						

◄ C A baby is left alone to beg for money

Millions of rural Chinese travel across China to find work in the city

Floods forced Ji Jianguo to leave his family farm in Anhui. He is one of 10 million small farmers who left their farms this year. They joined the 80 million who already live in shanty towns in China's cities.

Fifteen years ago 92% of the population were farmers. Now only 40% of people farm the land.

Chinese leaders blame migrants for crime and over-crowding in the cities. Migrants cannot become legal residents in the cities where they live. They may work there, but their children cannot go to school. They can get no health care. But China needs the migrants' cheap labour for its economic growth. Most low-paid jobs, like street-selling, are done by migrants.

▲ D Adapted from 'Baltimore Sun' by Ian Johnson, which appeared in *The Guardian* on 3 November 1994

> We do the work that no one else wants. I don't mind hard times here. It is still better than in my village. I have even saved enough to buy a TV for my parents back home.
>
> I get up at 4 a.m. and cycle to the wholesale market. I sell vegetables to other migrants who then sell them on the streets. Beijing residents don't want this work. We work outside in the sun and rain. It's hard, but anything is better than farming!

1 Use photos A and C. What do they show about:
  a) the good things industrial growth has brought
  b) the bad things industrial growth has brought?

2 Graph B shows the differences between manufacturing and **service industries** in Hong Kong.
  a) What type of industry is shown by:
    (i) the blue bars
    (ii) the red bars?
  b) What is the difference between what has happened to these two industries in Hong Kong?
  c) Why have jobs been lost in some industries in Hong Kong?

3 Use D and E.
  a) Give reasons for migrants moving to the cities.
  b) What effect does this have on rural areas?
  c) List the difficulties facing migrants when they move to the city.

▲ E **Deng Jiefang is a vegetable wholesaler in Beijing. He lives in one tiny room with his wife and son**

Review
- Countries in south-east Asia have moved away from selling primary commodities.
- They have built strong manufacturing industries. They export goods such as textiles, plastics, and electronics.
- Transnational companies have set up some of these firms.
- Economic success has brought both advantages and disadvantages.

4 Japan

Japan is a rich, developed country in east Asia.
- What are Japan's landscape and environment like?
- How does Japan cope with earthquakes?
- How has Japan become an economic superpower?

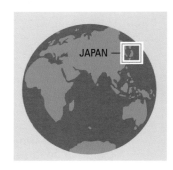

JAPAN

The Japanese landscape

Map A shows that Japan is made up of a long line of islands. They stretch over 1800km from north to south. Four large islands, Hokkaido, Honshu, Shikoku, and Kyushu make up 98% of Japan's land. Japan has 4000 smaller, volcanic islands.

Japan lies where four plates of the Earth's crust meet. Movement of the plates causes volcanic activity and earthquakes in Japan. There are 40 active volcanoes in Japan. Photo B shows the highest, Mount Fuji.

▼ A Japan

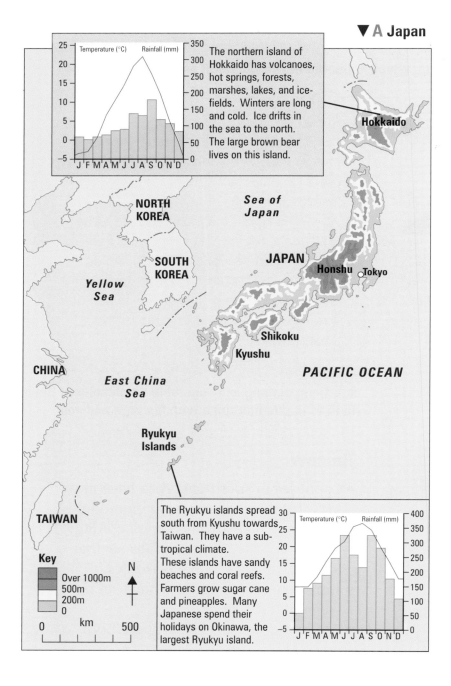

The northern island of Hokkaido has volcanoes, hot springs, forests, marshes, lakes, and ice-fields. Winters are long and cold. Ice drifts in the sea to the north. The large brown bear lives on this island.

Temperature (°C) Rainfall (mm)

NORTH KOREA

Sea of Japan

SOUTH KOREA

Yellow Sea

JAPAN

Honshu Tokyo

Hokkaido

Shikoku

Kyushu

CHINA

East China Sea

PACIFIC OCEAN

Ryukyu Islands

TAIWAN

Key

Over 1000m
500m
200m
0

N

0 km 500

The Ryukyu islands spread south from Kyushu towards Taiwan. They have a sub-tropical climate. These islands have sandy beaches and coral reefs. Farmers grow sugar cane and pineapples. Many Japanese spend their holidays on Okinawa, the largest Ryukyu island.

Temperature (°C) Rainfall (mm)

▼ B Mount Fuji

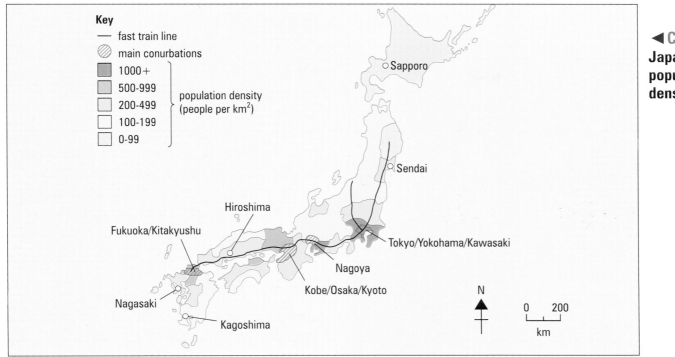

◄ C

Japan's population density

Urban Japan

Japan is a mountainous country. Cities, roads, and railways are crowded onto the flat coasts and valleys. So, while some parts of Japan are very densely populated, others are almost empty. For example, Tokyo's **population density** is 5430 per km². But in Hokkaido it is just 72 per km². Cities on the south-east coast have grown so much that they have joined up to form large urban areas or **conurbations**. These conurbations are shown on map C. They contain 45% of Japan's population.

1 Use map A.
  a) Name the four main Japanese islands from north to south.
  b) Which is the largest island?

2 Use map C to name the three most populated areas in Japan.

3 a) What is the average temperature in January in:
  (i) Hokkaido
  (ii) the Ryukyu islands?

  b) Give the average rainfall in June for these two places.
  c) Where would you rather take a holiday, Hokkaido or Ryukyu? Give your reasons.

4 Name two natural dangers in Japan.

5 a) In which part of Japan are most cities found?
  b) Give one reason for this.
  c) What is the name for an area where cities have grown so large that they join together?

Tokyo

A total of 40 million people live in, or close to, Tokyo. This is 32% of Japan's population. The city was mostly destroyed by an earthquake in 1923 and by bombing in 1945. Modern Tokyo was built quickly and with very little planning. Heavy industries, such as oil-refineries and chemical works, are on reclaimed land in Tokyo Bay. Smaller factories are mixed in with housing in the city centre. The suburbs spread up to 50km from the city centre.

Lack of space

Japanese homes are much smaller and more expensive than homes in Europe or America because land is so expensive. Land in central Tokyo costs US $93 000 per m^2. The problem of lack of space is solved in various ways:
- reclaiming land from the sea
- building skyscrapers
- building main roads on stilts
- building two or more levels underground.

▲ **A** An aerial view of Central Tokyo

Tenure	Japan	UK
Owner occupied	62	67
Rented (private)	25	7
Rented (company)	7	2
Local authority	6	20
Housing association	–	4

◄ **B** Housing in Japan

1 Use map C. Give four-figure references for:
 a) Tokyo thermal power plant
 b) Hama Detached Palace Garden.

2 Use map C to name points A, B, C, and D on photo A.

3 Use table B.
 a) Draw a divided bar graph to show the information in B.
 b) Copy out this sentence, filling in the gaps.
 In .... more people privately rent their home than in ....
 c) Write a sentence of your own to show another difference between housing in Japan and the UK.

4 Give one reason why Japanese homes are small.

5 List the ways in which space problems are solved in Japanese cities.

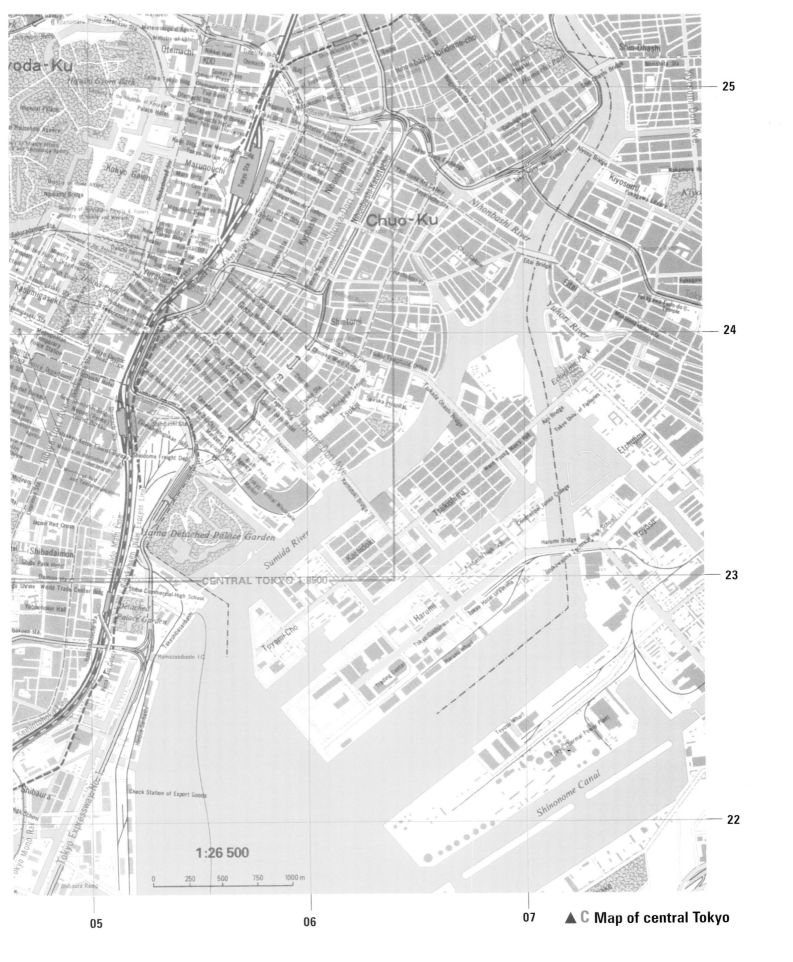

▲ **C Map of central Tokyo**

The Japanese and the environment

In the west, people feel strongly about environmental or 'green' issues. These issues are not so important to the Japanese. Greenpeace, for example, protests against Japan's whaling. Japan kills about 300 minke whales every year. The Japanese say it is for research but the whale meat is eaten in expensive restaurants. Japan imports more mahogany from tropical **rainforests** than any other country. The wood is used for furniture and disposable chopsticks. Most of the wood is logged using unsustainable methods, which means that the trees are not being replaced.

The throw-away society

Japan is a consumer society. People like to buy as many goods as possible. Goods often have too much packaging. Very few second-hand goods are sold. Even perfectly good cars are scrapped. About 45% of paper is recycled but used electrical goods are thrown away. The government now encourages manufacturers to make televisions, washing machines, and fridges that can be recycled easily.

◄ A Other countries protest because Japan still kills whales

▼ B **Aluminium used in Japan**

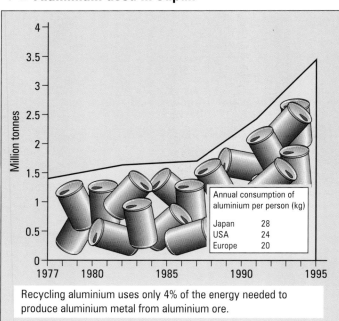

Annual consumption of aluminium per person (kg)

Japan	28
USA	24
Europe	20

Recycling aluminium uses only 4% of the energy needed to produce aluminium metal from aluminium ore.

▼ C **Waste produced in different countries**

Country	Waste produced (kg per person)		GNP per person (US $)
	1980	1990	1991
Austria	222	320	20 380
France	260	328	20 600
Greece	259	296	6 230
Japan	355	408	26 920
Portugal	214	287	5 620
Spain	270	322	12 460
Switzerland	351	441	33 510
UK	319	398	16 750
USA	723	803	22 560

Matsushita now makes a TV which can be taken apart by removing just four screws. Hitachi has a washing machine with a stainless steel tank, which can be recycled. Mitsubishi has cut down the number of different models it sells.

▲ D **Adapted from *Warmer Bulletin*, February 1995**

Living with earthquakes

Japan has 7500 earthquakes a year but most of these are too small for people to notice. Planners try to prevent earthquake damage by:

- building skyscrapers which will bend and flex during an earthquake
- building tall buildings with special foundations that soak up shock waves
- practising earthquake drill – on 1 September every year the entire population of Tokyo practises what to do in an earthquake.

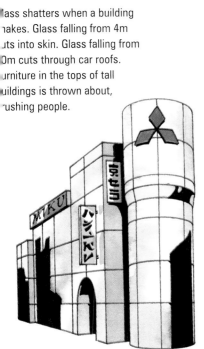

Glass shatters when a building shakes. Glass falling from 4m cuts into skin. Glass falling from 10m cuts through car roofs. Furniture in the tops of tall buildings is thrown about, crushing people.

Tremors can break gas pipes. Fires can start if people do not turn off their gas. As hot air from a fire rises, new air rushes in to feed the flames with fresh oxygen. This makes super-hot winds called a **fire storm**.

▼ E The problems caused by an earthquake

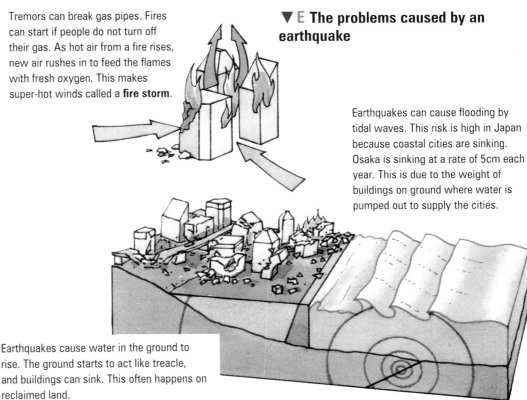

Earthquakes can cause flooding by tidal waves. This risk is high in Japan because coastal cities are sinking. Osaka is sinking at a rate of 5cm each year. This is due to the weight of buildings on ground where water is pumped out to supply the cities.

Earthquakes cause water in the ground to rise. The ground starts to act like treacle, and buildings can sink. This often happens on reclaimed land.

---

1 Why do people protest against Japan's whaling and use of hardwoods?

2 Look at table C. Which countries produce the most waste per person, the richer or the poorer ones?

3 Look at B. Why is it a good idea to recycle aluminium?

4 Read extract D. Explain how one product is being made so that it is more environmentally friendly.

5 Make a poster about *either* whaling in Japan *or* Japan's use of tropical hardwoods. Your poster should show people in Japan that the environment is important.

6 a) Describe the main dangers during an earthquake in Japan.
  b) How have planners tried to reduce the risk?

Kobe: diary of an earthquake

An earthquake recording 7.2 on the Richter scale hit the city of Kobe at 5.46 a.m. on 17 January 1995. Shock waves shook and split buildings, roads, gas, and water pipes. Raised roads collapsed. It was the worst earthquake in Japan since the one in Tokyo in 1923. More people would have died if the earthquake had happened during the rush hour. Thousands were killed in the fire storms which followed.

▶ **A The cause of the 1995 earthquake**

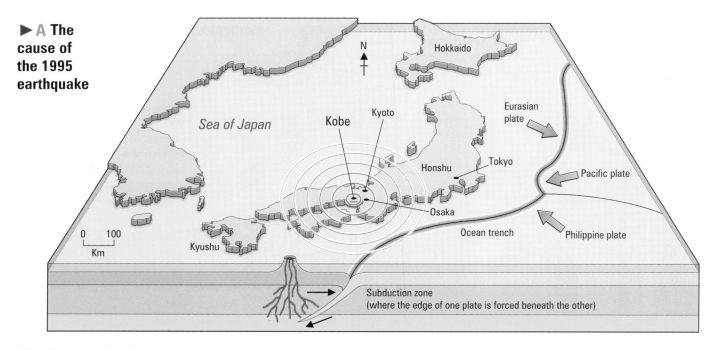

▼ **B Kobe before the earthquake**

▼ **C Kobe after the earthquake**

Earthquake terror

Japan's fears of a major earthquake came true today. A huge tremor shook cities, killing and injuring thousands of people.

'It was like the end of the world,' said 64-year-old Minoru Takasu. 'I wasn't injured because I hid between a cupboard and the wall.'

Japan is shocked that its new 'earthquake-proof' buildings and roads did not stand up to a major earthquake.

▲ D Adapted from *The Shropshire Star*, 17 January 1995

A city of ruins and ashes

Fires from broken gas pipes still burn in the ruins of Kobe. But thousands of people are suffering in the freezing cold. There is not enough room for everyone to shelter in schools and sports halls. So some homeless people are staying outside, trying to keep warm with small fires.

▲ E Adapted from the *Daily Telegraph*, 19 January 1995

17 Jan	1247
18 Jan	1800
19 Jan	3021
21 Jan	4412
30 Jan	5100
18 Feb	5390

▲ F The growing number of people killed

The cost of the earthquake

Kobe's port, which deals with 12% of Japan's exports, was closed. Matsushita, the largest producer of electronics in the world, closed its factories. Large steel and tyre factories also shut down. Earthquake damage cost 100 companies a total of US $10.4 billion. Other businesses tried to make money from the earthquake tragedy. One company put up the price of its roof tiles from 300 yen each (£2) to 5000 yen (£33).

Factfile: Kobe earthquake

- The earthquake hit Kobe at 5.46 a.m. on 17 January 1995.
- It measured 7.2 on the Richter scale.
- 5390 people were killed and 23 600 were injured.
- More than 40 800 buildings were destroyed or damaged.

1 a) Explain why there might have been more deaths in Kobe if the earthquake had struck during the rush hour.

b) What was the main cause of death in this earthquake?

2 List the problems facing the people who were made homeless by the earthquake.

3 Explain how businesses were affected by the earthquake.

4 What problems would the fire brigade and ambulance crews have had in helping people after the earthquake?

5 Table F shows that people died because of the earthquake weeks after it had struck. Suggest some possible reasons for this.

6 Use map A to name the three towns most affected by the 1995 earthquake.

High tech industry in Japan

Japan is the world's largest producer of semiconductors (microchips). These are used in electrical goods such as computers and in aircraft. But Japan now makes fewer TVs and video recorders than it did in the 1980s. China has overtaken Japan as the biggest producer of TVs. Japan now imports more TVs than it exports. This is because:

- Japan's products have become more expensive abroad
- countries with lower wages, like Malaysia and China, can make cheaper TVs and videos
- most people in Japan already own a TV and video recorder.

▲ B **Microchip factory, Osaka**

► C **Japan's changing electronics industry**

Export of electronic goods

Billion Yen

Source: Financial Times 02-11-94

Production of electronic goods

Billion Yen

Source: Financial Times 02-11-94

▼ A **Japan's electronics industry**

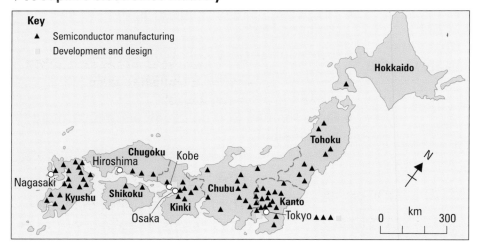

Key
▲ Semiconductor manufacturing
▢ Development and design

Hokkaido · Tohoku · Chugoku · Kobe · Hiroshima · Nagasaki · Kyushu · Shikoku · Kinki · Chubu · Kanto · Osaka · Tokyo

0 km 300

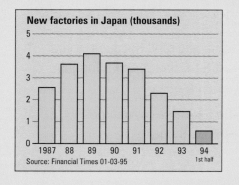

New factories in Japan (thousands)

1987 88 89 90 91 92 93 94
1st half
Source: Financial Times 01-03-95

Money spent by Japanese companies setting up branches abroad (billions of US dollars)

1987 88 89 90 91 92 93
Source: Financial Times 01-03-95

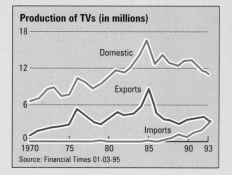

Production of TVs (in millions)

Domestic · Exports · Imports

1970 75 80 85 90 93
Source: Financial Times 01-03-95

Changes in Japanese technology

Some Japanese electronics firms have moved abroad. It is cheaper for them to make their goods abroad where wages are lower. It also makes it easier to sell them. The number of Japanese goods made abroad is growing steadily.

New products

Japan's electronics firms are making new products. Japanese firms use their skills to develop products which use new technologies. For example they now make wide screen TVs, which few foreign countries can produce. Sega, Nintendo, and Sony have recently redeveloped their hardware. New CD-based games are replacing cartridges that were used in the early 1990s. CDs are cheaper to make and store much more information. Now the customers get better games, and the companies get bigger profits.

> Labour costs in Japan are the highest in the world. Other costs, such as land, building, water, electricity, and shipping, are also the highest in the world.
>
> *Mr Harus Tsuji, President of Sharp*

> Technology is moving overseas. Now we are worried about the loss of simple skills.
>
> *Mr Minoru Saitoh*

▲ **D** Opinions about Japan's electronic industry in 1995

	Publishing	Manufacturing	Distribution and marketing	Retailer
PC/CD-ROM	37	8	15	40
Console cartridge	10	35	20	35

◄ **E** Where your money goes when you buy a computer game (percentages)

1 Give three examples of electronic products made in Japan.

2 Use map A. Describe the location of the electronics industry.

3 Use the graphs in C and the comments in D. In Japan what has been happening to:
  a) production of consumer electronics
  b) the export of electronic goods
  c) the number of new factories setting up in Japan
  d) money spent by Japanese firms on overseas factories?

4 a) Name one change in the Japanese electronics industry.
  b) Read the opinions in D. Give reasons for the changes in Japanese industry.

Did you know?

The Japanese games company, Sega, wants to build a virtual reality theme park, in Piccadilly Circus, London. Sega is the world leader in large electronic games and rides. It has a theme park, Joypolis, in Yokohama, Japan. Each year 1.5 million visitors go there to have fun with virtual reality headsets, space-flight games, and bumper cars.

Japanese people at work

Japan's economy is based on iron and steel, cars, and high tech industries like electronics. More people in Japan now work in service industries than in manufacturing, as graph A shows. Men usually have the best-paid jobs. The Japanese work long hours. They often work a thirteen-hour day, and on Saturday and Sunday as well. Workers feel they must stay at work until their boss goes home. To show that they are hard-working, workers won't take a holiday if the boss doesn't take his. It is thought that 10 000 Japanese die every year through overwork.

Japanese people at school

In Japanese schools learning is done by repeating what the teacher tells the pupils. Pupils are not asked for their opinions. Japanese children take many tests and exams, which they call *shiken jigoku* or 'exam hell'. They even take exams to get into infant classes. It is very hard to get to university but, once there, the work is easier. 'Many students hardly ever open a book,' said one Japanese student.

▼ A **How people are employed in Japan (percentages)**

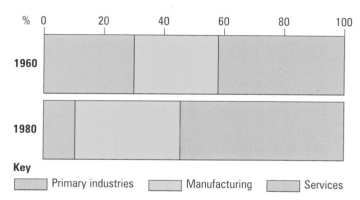

Key
Primary industries   Manufacturing   Services

▼ B **Rock and roll fans in Yoyogi Park**

1 Use the following figures to draw a divided bar graph of employment in Japan in 1995.
  ● primary industries 7%
  ● manufacturing 33%
  ● services 60%.

2 a) Use graph A. How did employment in Japan between 1960 and 1980 change in:
  a) primary industry
  b) manufacturing
  c) services?

3 Discuss:
  a) the problems school or work might cause in a Japanese family
  b) what people in the UK might learn from the Japanese way of working.

4 Look at graph C.
  a) Describe changes in Japan's population between 1950 and 1988 in the following groups:
    (i) people over 65
    (ii) children under fourteen.
  b) What further changes to these two groups are expected by the year 2040?

5 The 15–64 age group is labelled 'productive'. Discuss what this means.

6 Give two reasons for Japan's ageing population.

7 Look at D. Which country:
  a) had the *lowest* percentage of people over the age of 65 in 1950
  b) has the *highest* percentage of people over the age of 65 today
  c) is expected to have the highest percentage of people over 65 in 2020?

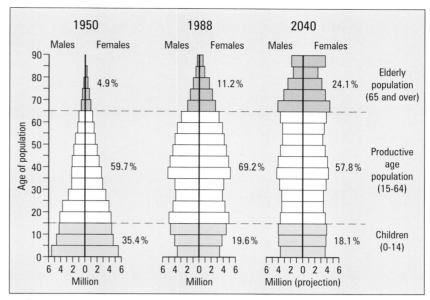

▲ C **How the Japanese population is ageing**

Japan's changing population

Graphs C and D show that Japan has an ageing population. After the Second World War family planning and birth control were encouraged because the Japanese government wanted to spend money on economic growth, not housing or education. The birth rate fell. Japanese families became richer during the 1960s and 1970s. People tended to marry later and have smaller families. This is partly due to the high cost of living and housing in Japan.

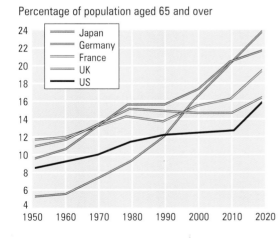

Percentage of population aged 65 and over

▲ D **Populations in different countries are changing at different rates**

Review
- Japan is mountainous so most people live on the crowded coastal plains.
- There is always a danger of volcanic eruptions and earthquakes because of the movement of the Earth's crust. The Kobe earthquake showed that disasters cannot always be prevented.
- Japanese people work very hard. They have built a strong economy but the ageing population and high labour costs may give problems in the future.
- Japan's technology leads the world. But it is behind other countries on green issues such as whaling.

We use energy to heat and light our homes, for power in factories, and for transport.
- **Which resources give us energy?**
- **How do different forms of energy affect the environment?**
- **How can we save energy?**

The energy we use

How many times in a day do you use something which uses electricity? Have you ever spent a day without electricity or gas? We all use different types of energy. Each day you use six times more energy than someone living in China, and sixteen times more energy than someone living in India. We also waste energy. Up to 65% of energy is lost or wasted. Diagram A gives an example: from 100 units of energy from coal, only four units are used to make light.

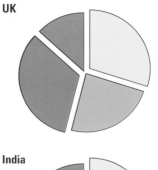

UK

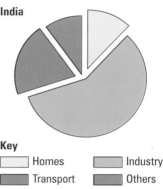

India

Key

Homes   Industry

Transport   Others

▲ **B Energy use in the UK and India (1990)**

▼ **A How the energy in coal is used to make light**

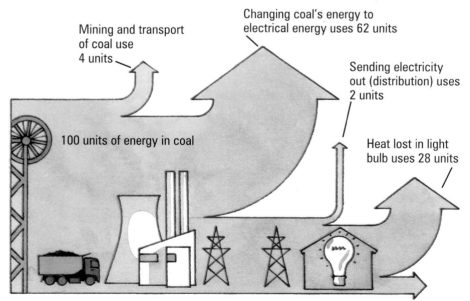

Mining and transport of coal use 4 units

Changing coal's energy to electrical energy uses 62 units

Sending electricity out (distribution) uses 2 units

100 units of energy in coal

Heat lost in light bulb uses 28 units

Only 4 units of energy are left to give light from light bulb

1 Work in pairs.
  a) List the things you have in your home which use energy.
  b) Split your list into:
   (i) things you could not do without
   (ii) luxuries that you could live without
   (iii) things that could use less energy.

2 Use diagram A.
  a) Where is most energy lost?
  b) What percentage of the energy in the coal is used to make light in the bulb?

Fossil fuels

Energy from **fossil fuels** is used to make 90% of electricity in the UK. Supplies of fossil fuels, like coal, gas, and oil, will not last forever. They can be used up. We say that they are **non-renewable**. The amount of fuel that is left is called a **fuel reserve**. Map D shows how much longer the world's fuel reserves may last.

▼ **C** **Energy used in the UK 1960–1993**

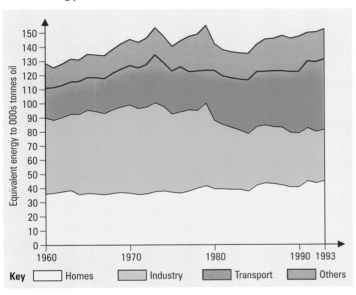

Key: Homes | Industry | Transport | Others

3 Use diagram B.
  a) What uses the largest amount of energy in:
    (i) the UK (ii) India?
  b) Give one other way in which energy use in India is different from in the UK.

4 Use diagram C. Which energy use has increased most?

5 Use map D.
  a) Which fuel has most years left?
  b) How is the Middle East different?

Country	% of world population	% of energy consumed
USA	4	24
India	16	2
China	22	8

6 This table shows that we do not all use the same amount of energy. Discuss why the USA uses more energy than India, yet has a smaller population.

▼ **D** **The world's fossil fuel reserves. The bars show how much fuel is left**

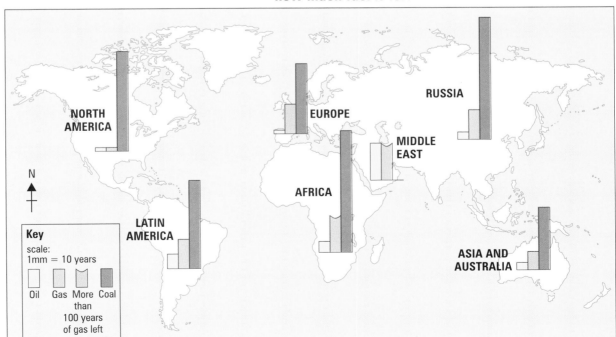

Energy and the environment

To understand what effect burning fossil fuels has, we need to know how the Earth's atmosphere works. The sun's energy passes through the Earth's atmosphere and warms the surface of the Earth. Heat is then radiated, or sent back out, from the Earth. Some of this heat is trapped in the atmosphere by greenhouse gases such as carbon dioxide (CO_2). This helps to keep the Earth warm. We call this the **greenhouse effect**.

Global warming

Burning fossil fuels adds extra carbon dioxide and other greenhouse gases to the atmosphere. This means that more heat will be trapped, and the Earth's atmosphere will become warmer. Gases from industry, vehicles, and farming make this problem worse. Scientists believe that temperatures over the whole world will rise. This is known as **global warming**. Ice caps could melt, making sea levels rise. Deserts could become hotter and drier.

▶ **A How pollution leads to global warming**

▼ **B Greenhouse gases**

Carbon dioxide	50%
CFCs	14%
Methane	18%
Nitrous oxide	6%
Surface ozone	12%

High levels of CO_2 from burning fossil fuels

Carbon dioxide and other gases in smoke

Atmosphere

Temperatures rise as heat is trapped by greenhouse gases

Rising temperatures melt snow and ice

Melting snow makes the seas rise

Some energy from the sun is sent back from the Earth

▼ **C Where greenhouse gases come from**

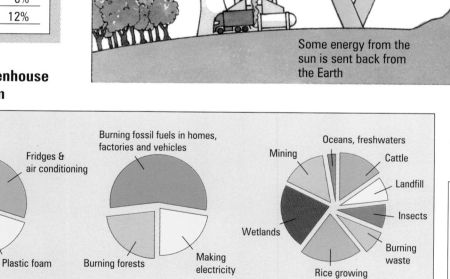

Sprays

Fridges & air conditioning

Solvents

Plastic foam

CFCs

Burning fossil fuels in homes, factories and vehicles

Burning forests

Making electricity

Carbon dioxide

Mining

Oceans, freshwaters

Cattle

Landfill

Insects

Wetlands

Rice growing

Burning waste

Methane

How much global warming is expected to make sea levels rise

▼ **D**

Predicted sea level rise (figures in cm)		
Year	Best estimate	Worst estimate
2000	5	8
2020	12	20
2040	25	40
2060	35	60
2080	48	85
2100	65	110

1 a) Use table B. Which gas is the most important for the greenhouse effect?

2 Use C. Which greenhouse gases are produced when energy is being used or made?

The effects of global warming

An increase in greenhouse gases will affect the world's climate. It will become hotter and there will be more storms. There will be more droughts and food shortages in the world's hot, dry areas. Sea levels may rise as ice caps melt. Map E shows possible changes in the temperatures around the world.

▼ **E** **How temperature may rise in different parts of the world**

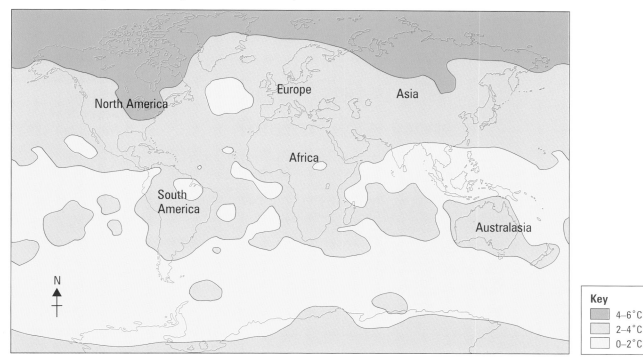

Key
- 4–6°C
- 2–4°C
- 0–2°C

3 a) Why is the greenhouse effect so important to the Earth's atmosphere?
  b) How could pollution lead to global warming?

4 Look at diagram A. Explain how a rise in greenhouse gases affects:
  a) global temperatures   **b)** sea levels.

5 Use map E and an atlas.
  a) In which part of the world will temperatures rise most?
  b) Name two countries where temperatures may rise by 2–4°C.

6 Use map F.
  a) List the towns which might flood.
  b) Why might it be difficult to travel from Ely to Cambridge?

▼ **F** **The Fens in East Anglia may flood if world temperatures rise**

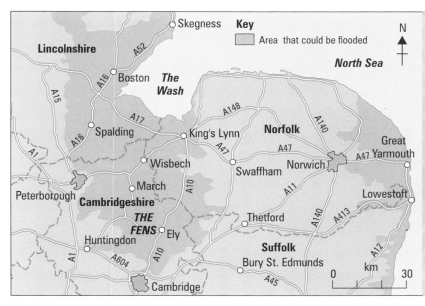

Key
- Area that could be flooded

Flooding on the coasts

A small rise in sea levels would affect low coastal areas such as East Anglia in the UK, Bangladesh, and the Netherlands. Most of the Seychelles in the Indian Ocean would be under water if the sea rose by only 45 cm. People on the tiny Pacific island of Tuvalu are afraid that global warming may bring floods.

▼ **A** The island of Tuvalu in the Pacific Ocean

◄ **B** Adapted from *The Independent*, 1 November 1992

Why is tiny Tuvalu angry with Britain?

Today Tuvalu is only about one metre above sea level. Storms already wash over the island. If the Earth becomes warmer and sea levels rise, Tuvalu may be completely covered by sea. The European Union is building barriers to protect the capital, Foangafale. The Dutch may build sea walls. But Britain is not helping.

► **C** Tarawa is a South Pacific island. Like Tuvalu, it may become covered by the sea if the sea levels rise

▼ **D** Trying to prevent flooding

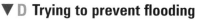

1 How is Tuvalu at risk from global warming?

2 Read extract B. Why is Tuvalu getting angry with Britain?

3 Describe the sea defence shown in photo D.

Coastal defences in the Netherlands

The Netherlands is a rich European country. Land reclaimed from the sea is now good farmland. Map F shows that some fields are already below sea level.

The Netherlands has a population of 15.4 million people. Nine million people live on land below sea level.

Sea defences have been built to protect the land. Large rocks are dropped off the coast to break up the waves. **Dykes**, or **embankments**, hold back the sea. Rock **groynes** trap the beach in front of the dyke. Photo E shows a barrage which has been built across a river mouth. These help to stop floods at high tide.

▲ E **A barrage built to prevent flooding in the Netherlands**

▼ F **The low-lying areas of the Netherlands**

4 Use map F.
   a) Name the cities which are below sea level.
   b) What percentage of land is at risk from flooding?

5 Give three ways in which farmland in the Netherlands is protected from flooding.

6 Look at photos D and E. How are the ways that Tuvalu and the Netherlands deal with the risk of flooding:
   a) similar
   b) different?

Nuclear power

Most of the UK's energy comes from fossil fuels. These are coal, gas, and oil. **Nuclear power** is the next most important source of energy. But many countries are cutting their plans for nuclear power. The USA, for example, has stopped building nuclear power stations. What are the problems of nuclear power?

Nuclear power in France

Nuclear power provides 75% of France's electricity. France has only small amounts of fossil fuels. Using nuclear fuel means that France needs to import less fossil fuels from other countries. It also means that France produces less carbon dioxide than most European countries.

Developing a nuclear industry was expensive – the French electricity company owed £25.4 billion in 1990.

▼ **A Sources of electricity in the UK and France**

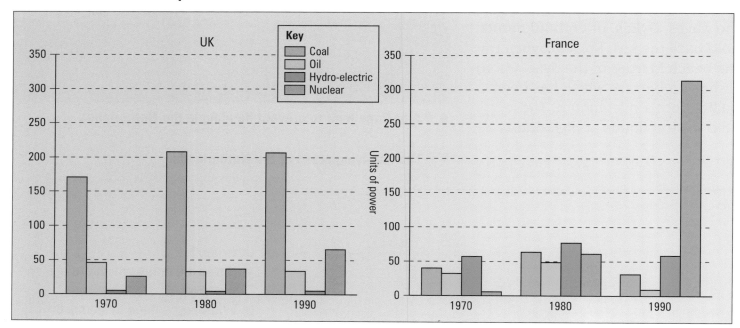

Problems of nuclear power in France

France relies heavily on nuclear fuel to make electricity. This has caused problems. During 1989–1990:
- design faults were found in several nuclear reactors
- a drought affected water supplies to nuclear plants as well as the amount of hydro-electricity that France could make.

France was forced to import electricity.

The nuclear power industry can harm the environment. It makes a lot of harmful, radioactive waste.

1 Use graph A.
  a) Which form of electricity is used most in:
    (i) the UK   (ii) France?
  b) How much of France's electricity came from nuclear power in:
    (i) 1970   (ii) 1980   (iii) 1990?

2 How has the development of nuclear power:
  a) helped France
  b) helped the environment
  c) caused problems for France?

International problems

In April 1986 there was an accident at a nuclear reactor at Chernobyl, in the Ukraine. An explosion blew radioactive material 5km into the atmosphere. Radioactivity spread across Europe as far as Greece, Scandinavia, and the UK. High levels of radioactivity are harmful both to people and the environment. Soil, people, and animals were badly affected locally as well as all over Europe. Many countries are now worried that the reactors in Russia and Eastern Europe may not be safe.

▲ **B The damaged nuclear reactor at Chernobyl**

Factfile: Chernobyl

- 31 people died immediately, others are still dying from illnesses caused by **radiation.**
- $10\,000km^2$ of land was poisoned by radioactivity.
- 220 villages are no longer safe for people to live in.
- 116 000 people fled their homes and 500 000 people were made homeless.

▼ **C The Austrian Environment Minister**

We decided not to use nuclear power. But we are worried about the safety of reactors across the border in the Czech Republic and Slovakia. We offered them free electricity if they close down their oldest reactors. We want our neighbours to join our 'nuclear free zone'.

▲ **D Nuclear plants in the Czech Republic and Slovakia**

3 a) List the problems caused by the explosion at Chernobyl.

b) Why is nuclear power an important issue for all countries, even for those who do not use it?

4 Use speech bubble C, map D, and the Factfile. Imagine that you live in Austria. Write a letter to the Energy Minister in the Czech Republic saying why you think the Republic should be declared a 'nuclear free zone'.

5 In pairs, discuss whether you think the French Energy Minister would want to join a nuclear free zone. Give your reasons.

Renewable energy

Renewable energy comes from things that do not run out. The wind, the sun, and water can give us energy which can be replaced. In the UK less than 1% of our energy comes from renewable sources. Some experts think that we could produce more renewable energy. By the year 2005 we could be making as much as 20% of our electricity from renewable sources. Electricity from wind power produces no waste and no greenhouse gases. The wind is free, and will not run out. But wind power still has problems. Each wind turbine makes only a small amount of electricity. Between 25 000 and 35 000 wind turbines would only produce 20% of the UK's electricity. Some people do not want the countryside to be covered with these turbines. They say that they are noisy and ugly.

Factfile: Renewable energy

- Wind – wind turbines can make electricity or pump water.
- Sun – solar panels use the sun's energy to heat water or generate electricity.
- Water – **hydro-electric power (HEP)** is made when water falls through a turbine. Look at photo A and diagram B.
- Sea power – the energy from the movement of waves can be used.
  Barrages built across an estuary could make electricity.
- Geothermal energy – water is pumped down deep holes in the ground. It is heated by hot rocks in the Earth's crust (see page 23).
- Energy from waste – heat or electricity can be made from burning waste. Methane gas from rotting waste can also be used.

1 Explain how the following can be used to make renewable energy:
a) the sun   **b)** wind   **c)** water.

2 Draw photo A. Use diagram B to help you label your drawing to show how the power station works.

▼ **A A hydro-electric power station in China**

▼ **B How a hydro-electric station works**

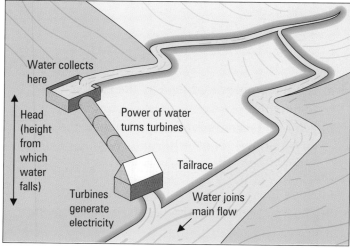

Water collects here

Head (height from which water falls)

Power of water turns turbines

Turbines generate electricity

Tailrace

Water joins main flow

3 List the good points and the bad points of wind energy.

Energy from waste

In the UK, 87% of household rubbish goes into **landfill** sites. Diagram D shows how dumping rubbish can harm the environment. Instead of throwing our rubbish away we could use it to make electricity.

- Household and industrial waste can be burnt to make hot water or electricity.
- Methane, or biogas, is made when things rot without oxygen. It is found in sewage works, farm manure, and in landfill sites. Methane can be burnt to give heat or electricity.

Fuel for cooking

In Gujarat, India, people cook on wood fires. Women collect wood from the forest but **deforestation** means that they must walk a long way to find wood. Biogas plants, such as one in Methan, Gujarat now give energy for cooking instead. You can read more about biogas plants on the next page.

▲ **C** Waste from this landfill site flows along the ditch into a tank

Landfill	83%
Incineration (burning)	7%
Recycling	5%
Landfill producing biogas	3%
Burning waste produces energy	2%

▲ **E** Getting rid of household waste

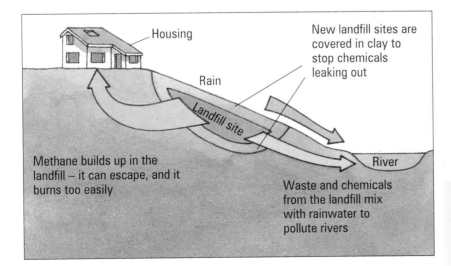

Housing

New landfill sites are covered in clay to stop chemicals leaking out

Rain

Landfill site

Methane builds up in the landfill – it can escape, and it burns too easily

River

Waste and chemicals from the landfill mix with rainwater to pollute rivers

▲ **D** Dangers to the environment from landfill sites

4 a) Where does biogas come from?
b) How can biogas be used?

5 Use D. How does biogas cause problems?

Case study: a biogas project

The biogas plant in Methan, Gujarat is run by the villagers. Members of the project who have cows collect manure. This ferments in a chamber and produces methane gas. The gas is used for cooking. Waste from the chamber is used to fertilize the crops.

▲ B Biogas project in Methan, India

▶ A

It was hard to get people to bring manure to the gas plant. People did not think the waste left in the chamber would be good for their crops. They wanted to keep taking free wood, rather than pay to join the project.

But it is better for the women and children now. No more smoky kitchens, coughs, or burning eyes! No hours spent looking for wood!

▼ C Villagers collecting manure for the biogas project

▶ D Inside a biogas plant

▼ E Cooking using wood and biogas

WOOD

BIOGAS

1 To explain how the biogas project works, copy the sentences and fill in the gaps.

   .... is collected. It .... in a chamber to produce .... gas. This gas is used for .... Solid waste left in the chambers is used to........ crops.

2 What problems does the use of firewood cause for:
   a) women   b) the environment.

3 How has the biogas project helped:
   a) the villagers b) the environment?

4 Look at photo E. Would you rather cook with biogas or firewood? Give reasons for your answer.

Saving energy

We can find ways to make better use of energy. Energy is often wasted. We can save energy by recycling things, such as aluminium cans or glass bottles. It takes 25 times less energy to recycle an aluminium can than it does to make a new one. Energy can also be saved around the house. Photo F shows how energy is lost from a house. Diagram G shows how to reduce such energy loss. Photo H shows a house built to use energy carefully.

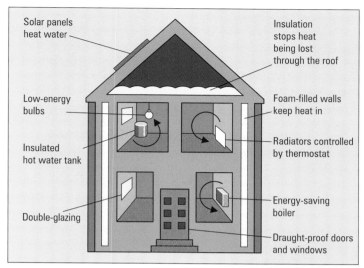

▲ **G How to cut down energy loss**

▲ **F Energy lost from a house. Red shows the areas where most heat is lost. Blue shows the areas that keep the most warmth in**

▲ **H Energy-saving house, front and back**

5 Use photo F and diagram G.
  a) Where is most heat lost in F?
  b) What can be done to reduce heat loss in this area?
  c) What part of house F loses little heat?
  d) How might this have been achieved?

6 a) Discuss the use of energy in your school.
  b) List the ways that energy might be wasted.
  c) List the ways that energy might be saved.

Review

- Energy is a very important resource.
- Fossil fuels can be used up so we must start using renewable types of energy.
- When we produce energy we must know how it affects the environment.
- We must make the most of the energy we produce, and reduce energy loss.

Many countries build huge dams. They control rivers and give water for irrigation schemes.
- **Why are these superdams built?**
- **How do superdams affect people and the environment?**
- **Why might smaller projects be better?**

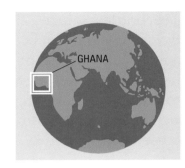

GHANA

Why do we need superdams?

Dams can control flooding. Some rivers flood after heavy rain, causing death and damage. Dams trap flood waters when the rivers are high. When the danger of floods has passed the water is let out. Dams also:
- give hydro-electric power
- supply water for farming, industry, and homes.

The Hoover Dam, in the USA, was the world's first **superdam**. Many other countries now have superdams.

▲ **A** The Akosombo Dam, Ghana

Location	No.
Canada	1
Latin America	17
China	7
East and south-east Asia	8
Turkey	1
India	4
Europe	4
USSR	2
Africa	4

▲ **B** Superdams being built in 1990

1 Use table B to draw a bar graph of superdams being built. Then cut and paste your bars onto a world map.

2 Are superdams being built, in developed or developing countries? Why do you think this is?

Case study: Akosombo superdam

Akosombo superdam was built on the River Volta in Ghana. In 1964 it cost US $120 million to build. Its aim was to produce hydro-electricity for Ghana's aluminium industry. Bauxite, or aluminium ore, is treated at a **smelter** in the port of Tema. Treating the aluminium uses 70% of the dam's electricity. Ghana's aluminium is exported to the USA.

The effects of the Akosombo dam
- 99% of Ghana's electricity comes from the dam.
- Spare electricity is sold to Togo, Benin, and the Ivory Coast.
- Water from Lake Volta is used to **irrigate** dry land to the north.
- Lake Volta now has a large fishing industry.

Since the dam was built, the coasts of Ghana and Togo have been eroded. Most of Keta, in Ghana, has fallen into the sea and coastal roads in Togo have been washed away. Protecting the coast with rock groynes would cost US $ 2–3 million per kilometre.

▲ **C Ghana**

3 a) Name two tributaries of Lake Volta.
  b) Measure the length of the lake from Tamale to the Akosombo dam.

4 Use map C and diagram D.
  a) How has the building of the dam caused coastal erosion?
  b) Name one town in Ghana and one in Togo that may suffer from coastal erosion.

5 Make a table to show the effects of the Akosombo dam.

	Good points	Bad points
Ghana		
Togo and Benin		

▼ **D How the Akosombo dam affects the coast**

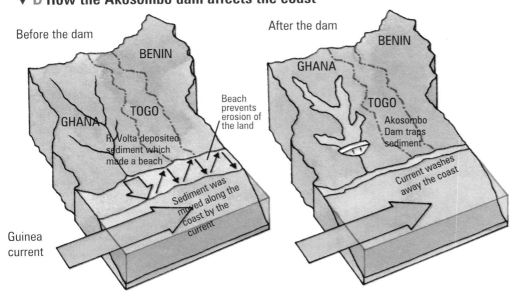

Case study: the Three Gorges Dam in China

The Three Gorges Dam is being built on the huge Yangtze River in China. 75 million people live on the Yangtze flood plain. The Yangtze river is dangerous. When it flooded in July 1995:

- 100 million people were affected
- 1 million homes were destroyed
- over 1000 people died.

The flooding was caused by heavy rain, melting snows, and deforestation. Diagram C shows how deforestation can cause heavy floods. These floods gave people a good reason to finish the Three Gorges Dam.

▲ **A These Yangtze gorges will fill with water when the dam is built**

1 Use map B and an atlas to name:
  a) the river that flows into the Yellow Sea
  b) the river that flows into the sea near Hong Kong.

2 Use B. Copy these sentences and fill in the gaps. *The aims of the Three Gorges project are to control the river and to prevent .... It will also generate .... and provide water for .... It will also make river .... easier.*

3 Give two ways in which the Three Gorges Dam project will improve people's lives.

▶ **B Flooding on China's major rivers**

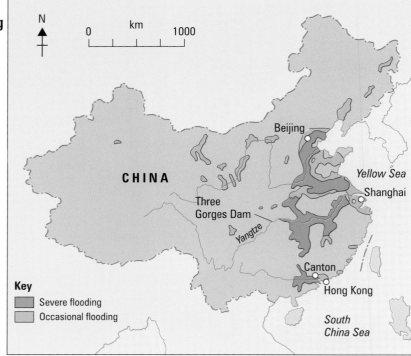

Key
- Severe flooding
- Occasional flooding

The aims of the Three Gorges Dam project:

1. To prevent flooding.
   Floods happen about every ten years on the Yangtze River. In 1935 a flood killed 142 000 people. The basin of the Yangtze River produces 40% of China's industrial and agricultural goods. Preventing floods is very important for China's economy.
2. To make hydro-electric power.
   The Three Gorges Dam should generate 18% of China's energy needs.
3. To give water for irrigation.
   Since the 1980s Chinese people have been giving up farming and moving to the cities. Life for farmers will be better if they can irrigate their crops. They will grow cash crops, like flowers to sell, not just food to live on.
4. To make river transport easier.
   The Yangtze flows down a **gorge** which is 660 km long. It drops down 139 rapids. When the **reservoir** is full these rapids will be flooded to a safe depth. Large ships will be able to use the river. This could cut transport costs by 35%.

How will the Three Gorges Dam affect people?

The Three Gorges Dam will flood 632 km² of land, including farmland, and two cities. Over 1 million people will need new homes. This worries the local people. Where will they live and work?

What effects will the dam have on the environment?

The water level in the gorges will rise by 40 m. This may ruin the beauty of the landscape.

The freshwater dolphin may be unable to live in the fast waters below the dam. The dam wall will stop the rare Chinese sturgeon fish reaching the part of the river where it lays its eggs.

Diagram C shows that **soil erosion** occurs as forests are cleared. People who are moved to new homes because of the dam will cut down more trees for fuel and farm land. This will erode the soil.

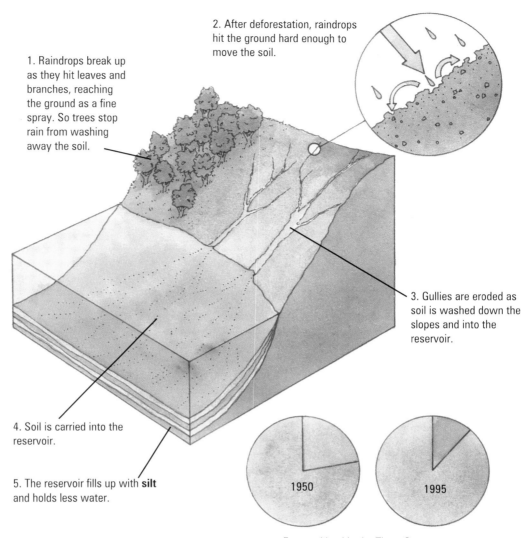

2. After deforestation, raindrops hit the ground hard enough to move the soil.

1. Raindrops break up as they hit leaves and branches, reaching the ground as a fine spray. So trees stop rain from washing away the soil.

3. Gullies are eroded as soil is washed down the slopes and into the reservoir.

4. Soil is carried into the reservoir.

5. The reservoir fills up with **silt** and holds less water.

1950

1995

Forested land in the Three Gorges area

▲ C The effects of deforestation

4 List the problems that the dam will cause:
   a) for people   **b)** for the environment.

5 Use diagram C. Explain how:
   a) trees prevent soil erosion
   b) the loss of trees causes soil erosion.

6 Working in groups list, in order of importance, reasons:
   a) for the dam   **b)** against the dam.

7 Judging from your lists, do you think it is a good idea to build the dam? Give your reasons.

Are there alternatives to superdams?

Can water for irrigation and hydro-electricity be provided without moving thousands of people or damaging the environment?

Small-scale solutions to water shortage

Adgaon is a village in Maharashtra, India. The Narmada superdam is planned 240 km to the north. Only 500 mm of rain falls in Adgaon during the rainy season. This often falls in just ten days. The village suffers from lack of water in the dry season, and soil erosion in the rainy season.

Appropriate technology

The villagers have built small earth dams across the streams. They have helped themselves using **appropriate technology**. This means that local people worked using local tools, methods, and materials. The dams were cheap and easy to build. They store water for use in **irrigation** during the dry season. Once all the water has been used, farmers take the silt which has been trapped by the dams to improve their soil.

The villagers have also made earth walls or **bunds** across their fields. These trap rainwater so that it soaks into the soil. Since less water runs over the soil, *bunds* also prevent soil erosion. Photo D shows how *bunds* are being used in other dry areas, like the Sahel on the edge of the Sahara.

The efforts of the villagers have made life in Adgaon better. Their wells now have water. Acacia, eucalyptus, and banana trees are now growing there.

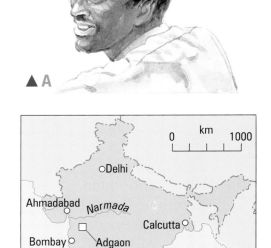

Large projects which need a lot of money are not helpful to developing countries like India. Countries should find ways which need less money and involve local people.

▲ A

▲ B Location of Adgaon, India

◄ C Using appropriate technology to build an earth dam in Adgaon, India

Region	Area	Area affected by erosion
North	150.6	40.7
Sahel	802.4	224.0
South	295.0	58.7
Others	38.0	8.9
Total	1286.0	332.3

▲ F **Soil erosion in Africa (millions of hectares)**

▲ D **Villagers are being shown how *bunds* work. Full size *bunds* are much larger**

Small-scale ways to use water

- Crops can be grown in hollows which collect rainwater around the plant.
- Hillsides can be terraced into strips of flat land for crops. This helps to stop soil erosion.
- Simple wells and pumps can use underground water or water from local streams.

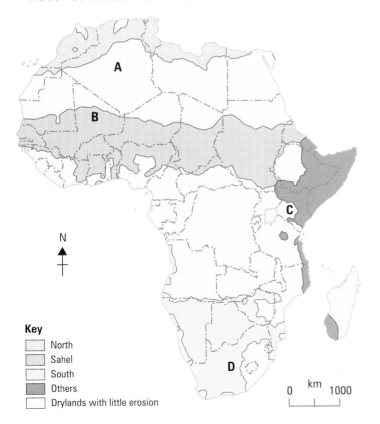

Key
- North
- Sahel
- South
- Others
- Drylands with little erosion

N

0 km 1000

▲ E **Dry regions of Africa**

1 Why does Adgaon have problems with its water supply?

2 a) Name two ways in which the people of Adgaon have solved their water problem.
  b) Copy this sentence and fill in the gaps.

  Bunds are small .... built across .... to store water. The water is used for farming and ..... . When the water is gone, the silt is used as ....
  c) Why are these small projects better for local people than superdams?

3 Use map E and an atlas. Name countries A–D.

4 Use table F. Draw bar graphs to show:
  a) the area of land in each region
  b) the area of land affected by soil erosion.

5 Use your bar graph to name the region:
  a) with the largest area of soil erosion
  b) with the largest proportion of land affected.

Small-scale ways to provide energy

In China, the government helps local, rural people to build small hydro-electric power stations. These are cheaper to build than superdams but the electricity they make is a little more expensive. These power stations help to reduce local power shortages but they cannot make large amounts of electricity.

Damming the Narmada River

India gets 28% of its electricity from hydro-electric power. As the country's economy grows, it needs more electricity. The Indian government wants to build two superdams on the Narmada River, one at Sadar Sarovar, the other at Narmada Sagar. They will also build 30 more large dams, 130 medium ones and 3000 minor ones along the river and its tributaries.

The aims of the Narmada project

The Indian government wants the project to:

- send water to Gujarat, a dry area with a population of 20 million people
- provide water and cheap electricity to help industry in Gujarat
- protect 750 000 people from floods.

West Gujarat	Jan	Feb	Mar	Apr	May	Jun	Jul	Aug	Sep	Oct	Nov	Dec
Temp (°C)	19	20	24	27.5	30	31	30	29.5	28	27.5	24	20
Rainfall (mm)	13	10	7	3	3	18	81	40	13	3	3	7
Nagpur	Jan	Feb	Mar	Apr	May	Jun	Jul	Aug	Sep	Oct	Nov	Dec
Temp (°C)	21	24	28.5	32.5	35	32	27.5	27	27.5	26	22.5	20
Rainfall (mm)	10	18	15	15	20	224	370	290	203	56	20	13

◀ **B Climate data**

▶ **C Climate in Ahmadabad, Gujarat**

▼ **A The Narmada River basin**

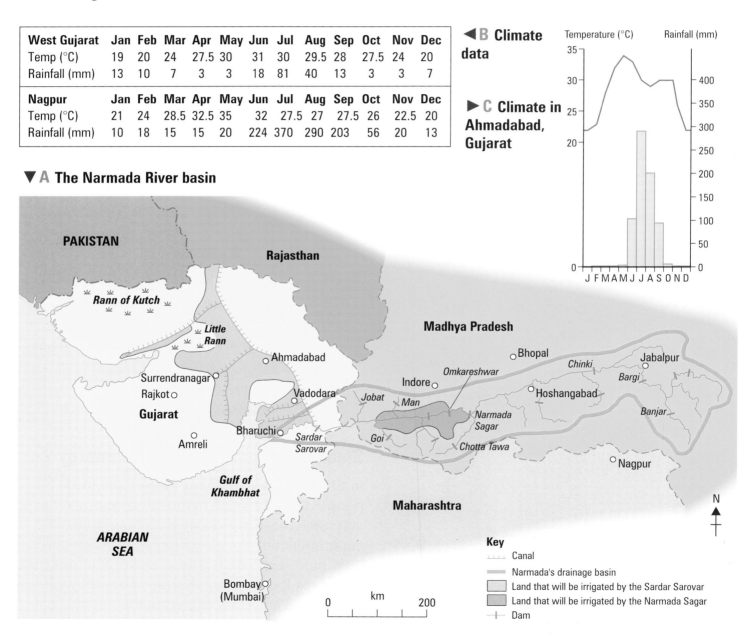

Key
- Canal
- Narmada's drainage basin
- Land that will be irrigated by the Sardar Sarovar
- Land that will be irrigated by the Narmada Sagar
- Dam

km
0   200

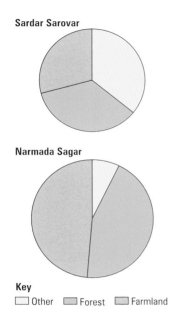

Sardar Sarovar

Narmada Sagar

Key
☐ Other ☐ Forest ☐ Farmland

▲ **D** **The area that the superdams will cover in water**

◄ **E** **The Sardar Sarovar dam at 60 m high. It will be 120 m tall when it is finished**

The issues in Gujarat

The Sardar Sarovar reservoir should help the dry state of Gujarat. Canals will carry water from the reservoir to drought areas. Some people are afraid that the canals will only take water to the rich farmers in the cotton-growing areas and not to the poor rural communities. The canals are also very expensive to build.

The issues in Madhya Pradesh

Up to 1.5 million people will lose their homes when land is flooded by the dam. Local people are afraid that they will not be given new homes and jobs. The Narmada Sagar reservoir will cover 90 000 hectares of land. Yet only 123 000 hectares will be irrigated. Deforestation will lead to soil erosion. Soil erosion will silt up the reservoirs.

---

1 Use map A. Copy and complete this sentence.

The Narmada flows through the Indian states of .... and .... It flows into the Gulf of .... at ....

2 Which state will have:
   a) most dams on the Narmada
   b) most land irrigated by the Narmada project?

3 Use the pie charts in D. Which of the two superdams will cover with water:
   a) most farmland?

b) 35% forest?

4 a) Use table B to draw a climate graph for Nagpur.
   b) Compare your graph with climate graph C. Which region has most rain?
   c) What do the graphs tell you about the need for the Sardar Sarovar dam?

5 Explain how the Narmada project will affect:
   a) people
   b) the environment.

Views on the Narmada project

▲ **A** People have strong feelings about the Narmada project

▼ **B** Changes in India's economy

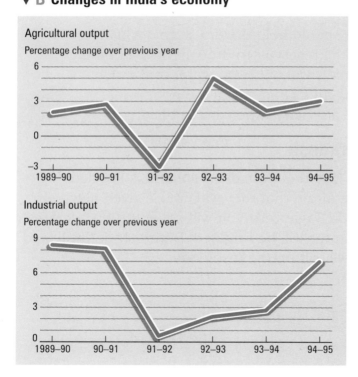

1 Use the graphs in B. Is India's economy increasing or decreasing?

2 Look at table C. Which type of electricity production in India has shown:
a) most growth since 1950
b) least growth since 1950?

Economic reasons

India already has fourteen superdams but more electricity is still needed. Power cuts are common. The Indian economy is growing fast and exports are increasing. More power is needed or the economy will not be able to grow. The Government hopes that large projects like Narmada will help poor people in the long run. They hope that a strong economy will bring more jobs and wealth for everyone, whether they are rich or poor.

▼ **C** Amount of electricity generated in India (billions kilowatt-hours)

Year	HEP	Thermal	Nuclear	Biogas projects	Total
1950–51	2.5	2.6	-	1.5	6.6
1960–61	7.8	9.1	-	3.2	20.1
1970–71	25.2	28.2	2.4	5.4	61.2
1980–81	46.5	61.3	3.0	8.4	119.2
1990–91	71.7	186.8	6.1	24.1	288.7
1991–92	72.5	208.6	5.6	27.5	314.2
1992–93	69.8	224.4	6.7	30.0	330.9

The rights of tribal peoples

The Narmada project will flood 3500 km^2 of forest and 600 km^2 of farmland. Up to 1.5 million people will lose their homes. They are mostly tribal people like Bhils, Pardhans, and Kols. Their traditional way of life is fishing, forestry, and farming. Each family will be given five hectares of new land. But this land is poor, and far from the river. Over-grazing and deforestation of this drier land will cause soil erosion.

Some tribal people have already moved and work in cotton factories. They earn money but they have lost their traditional way of life. Tribal people are angry that dams damage their people instead of helping them. Some even say they would rather drown on their land than leave.

Effects on the environment in Gujarat

The Sardar Sarovar dam will send irrigation water to Gujarat. Scientists fear that irrigation will make the water table rise. The soil will become waterlogged and plants will die. All water contains small amounts of salts. Irrigation increases these amounts. As diagram D shows, making water salty, or **salination**, eventually makes the soil useless for farming.

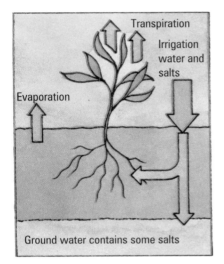

Transpiration

Irrigation water and salts

Evaporation

Ground water contains some salts

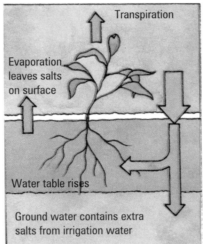

Transpiration

Evaporation leaves salts on surface

Water table rises

Ground water contains extra salts from irrigation water

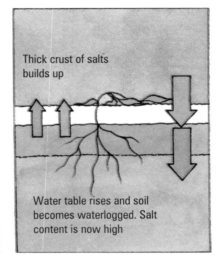

Thick crust of salts builds up

Water table rises and soil becomes waterlogged. Salt content is now high

◀ **D How irrigation can lead to salination**

Dams and asses

A study by India's Wildlife Institute shows that the canals will damage the salt flats of Little Rann of Kutch (LRK). Many canals will pass near by or through the LRK, which is home to many wild asses. Soil will become waterlogged. This will kill the plants which are adapted to dry, salty conditions. Animals such as blackbuck, desert fox, and spiny-tailed lizards will be affected.

E Adapted from *BBC Wildlife*, March 1995

Review

- Superdams are being built in many developing countries.

- They generate power, provide water, control flooding.

- Small-scale schemes cost less, and use less land. The local people do not lose their homes, or way of life. Wildlife is also protected.

3 a) What reasons does the Indian government give for the Narmada project?
b) Why do people protest against the project?

4 How will the dam affect:
a) the environment
b) people?

5 Use diagram D to explain how irrigation can damage plants.

6 Make a leaflet or poster to protest about the Narmada Dam. It should explain the problems for people and the environment.

7 Use the information in this unit to write about the advantages of superdams.

Ecotourism

Worldwide, 204 million people work in tourism. As tourism grows it affects the natural environment.
- **Can the environment be protected while tourism grows?**
- **Is ecotourism helpful to the tourist industry and the environment?**

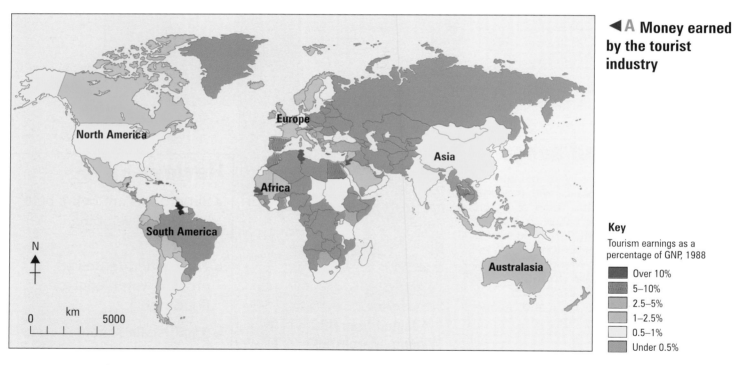

◀ **A** Money earned by the tourist industry

North America

Europe

Asia

Africa

South America

Australasia

N

0   km   5000

Key

Tourism earnings as a percentage of GNP, 1988

■	Over 10%
■	5–10%
■	2.5–5%
■	1–2.5%
□	0.5–1%
■	Under 0.5%

Global tourism

The tourist industry is the world's biggest employer. One in nine jobs in the world is in tourism. Tourism creates jobs and wealth but it can also create problems. Millions of tourists travel to all parts of the world. They affect fragile environments such as rainforests and **coral reefs**. But do local people gain from tourism?

1 Use map A and an atlas. Name one country that gets more than 5% of its GNP from tourism in:
 a) North Africa
 b) Europe
 c) Central America.

2 What percentage of income comes from tourism in:
 a) Kenya   **b)** India
 c) Sri Lanka   **d)** Brazil?

GOA

Goa's wonderful white beaches make it perfect for peaceful holidays. It is full of beautiful scenery and interesting forts, churches, mosques, and temples. Indian people are polite and helpful. You always feel welcome in relaxed Goa.

▲ **B** Adapted from Thomson's *Worldwide* brochure

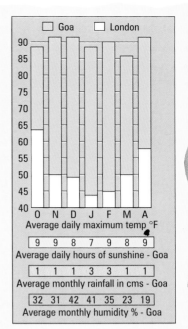

Average daily maximum temp °F

	O	N	D	J	F	M	A
Average daily hours of sunshine - Goa	9	9	8	7	9	8	9
Average monthly rainfall in cms - Goa	1	1	1	3	3	1	1
Average monthly humidity % - Goa	32	31	42	41	35	23	19

Too many tourists?

Countries want tourists because they provide jobs and money for local people. But, as the numbers of tourists rise, the needs of local people and the environment can be forgotten. Small resorts become overgrown and ugly, spoiling the places tourists come to see. **Mass tourism**, when many tourists visit the same place, can harm the environment. Goa, in India, suffers from mass tourism. Nearly half of all visitors to India stay in Goa. The fast growth of hotels has caused problems, as extract C shows.

▶ **C** Adapted from *The Independent on Sunday*, 12 February 1995

Mass tourism poisons paradise

Visitors to Goa enjoy its mix of Portuguese and Indian culture. They visit its sandy beaches. By the end of the century five million tourists will have been to Goa. But tourist development could destroy both Goa's culture and environment. Greedy hotel owners aim to get rich from the growing tourist trade. Hotels are built on beaches without planning permission. Mangroves and wetlands have been drained and trees cut down. Sewage is spilt onto beaches and rice fields.

3 What is mass tourism?

4 Read extract B.
   a) Give three reasons why you might wish to visit Goa as a tourist.
   b) If you lived in London, in which month would you most like to visit Goa? Give your reasons.

5 Read about tourism in Goa. Copy and complete this table.

	Tourism in Goa	
	Good points	Bad points
For local people		
For the environment		

Belize: tourism and the environment

Belize is a small country in Central America. Tourism is now the fastest growing part of Belize's economy. Tourists are attracted by the tropical climate, beaches, and local history. It also has the second largest barrier reef in the world. Belize wants to develop small-scale tourist projects which aim to look after the environment. This is known as **ecotourism**.

Mangroves

Mangrove trees grow near coasts where fresh river water mixes with sea water. All around the world mangroves are being cut down. The wet land is drained. Tourist resorts are often built on this land. Should Belize do the same?

▲ A **Mangrove lost around the world**

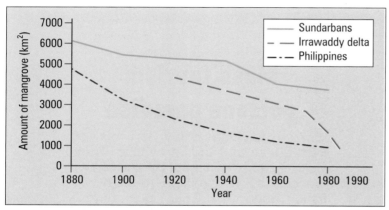

Mangroves give a home to animals such as howler monkeys, deer, crocodile, snakes, and crabs.

Mangrove roots hold the mud together – protecting the land from erosion.

Large roots support the tree above high tide. They trap and hold sediment.

Mangrove timber can be a valuable resource.

Mangroves provide breeding grounds for fish, and nesting areas for birds.

▲ B **Why mangroves are important**

▼ C **Belize, in central America**

km
0   30

N

Corozal Town

Ambergris Cay

Ho Chan
Marine Park

Bermudian
Landing

**Belize
City**

Belmopan

Area in
satellite photo E

Punta Gorda

Key

Forest reserves   Bird reserves   —— Roads
Coral reef   Other wildlife reserves

High tech ways to protect the environment

If we know where they can be found, rare wildlife areas can be protected. For twenty years, geographers from Edinburgh University have worked with the government of Belize to map the country's vegetation. Storyboard D shows how this is done. With this information, the Belize government has set up nature reserves, wildlife parks, and **conservation** areas. This has helped the growth of tourism, and has saved many areas of mangrove.

◄ D

1 Satellites take photos of Belize.

2 Colours on the photos are matched up with vegetation in just a few places. It is then quick and cheap to work out what is growing everywhere.

3 Computers use the satellite photos to make vegetation maps of Belize. Rare habitats can be mapped and protected.

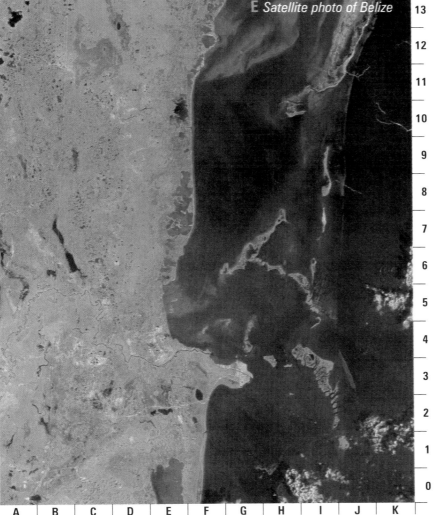

E *Satellite photo of Belize*

1 Use map C.
  a) How long is the Belize coral reef?
  b) What percentage of Belize is forest reserve: 10%, 20%, or 50%?

2 Use graph A. Which area is losing its mangroves at the fastest rate?

3 List the reasons why mangrove swamps are worth protecting.

4 Use map C and photo E. Match grid references to these places:
  B3   Ambergris Cay
  G3   shallow water
  G12 Belize city
  J11 forest.

5 Explain why the scientists use satellites instead of doing all the survey on foot.

▲ **A** Tourists enjoy visiting Mayan temples in Belize

The needs of local people

Of the population of Belize, 9% are Mayan Indians. Photo A shows a temple built by Mayan people hundreds of years ago. Today Mayans are farmers who grow maize and vegetables. Their 'slash and burn' farming makes small clearings in the rainforest. It gives the forest a pattern of growth and regrowth. If farmers cut down more forest, animals such as the black howler monkey will lose their homes. Can Mayans improve their life without losing their culture or harming the rainforest? One answer may be ecotourism.

The Bermudian Landing project

The rainforest home of the black howler monkey was under threat at Bermuda Landing. Land was being cleared for farming. Local Mayans are trying ecotourism to save the forest. They are developing tourism carefully so that their environment is protected.

- Farmers leave thick bands of forest around their fields. This has helped the black howler monkeys. Their population has grown by 30%.
- A monkey sanctuary was created. It is visited by 3000 tourists each year.
- Tourists stay with local families for a small fee. They wash in the river, and fetch drinking water from wells. There is no hotel.

Lucky Belize

Ecotourism in Belize means looking after the reefs, rainforest wildlife, and Mayan ruins. Tourists come to see these things so the environment must stay unspoilt. But people need jobs, so tourism and agriculture have to develop. This means that sometimes, a few areas of mangroves or eel grass must be given up.

▲ **B** Adapted from *The Belize Review*, June 1990

▼ **C** A black howler monkey

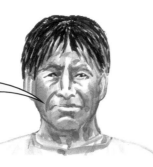

▼ E Mayan people are developing ecotourism

Tourists have an adventure staying here. They learn about our way of life.

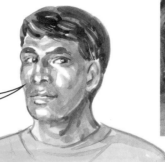

Tourists used to bring packed lunches. We had no way of getting rid of their litter. Now the visitors eat lunch with families in the village. They enjoy it!

▲ D A Mayan Indian village

Invited tourists only!

The Quichua people in Ecuador are doing something unusual. To protect their way of life and their rainforest, they are inviting tourists. But they only invite environmental groups and students who are seriously interested in protecting the rainforest. The Quichua teach them about the importance of the rainforest. By doing this they hope to protect the rainforest and to keep their community together. They also hope to build a new school and health centre so that their standard of living will improve.

► F Adapted from *Common Cause*, 1993

1 What is meant by ecotourism?

2 How has the ecotourism project at Bermuda Landing helped:
   a) local people
   b) wildlife and the environment?

3 How did the Mayans:
   a) avoid building hotels
   b) stop the problem of litter?

4 Read extract F. How is the Bermuda Landing project similar to the project run by the Quichua people in Ecuador?

5 Imagine you live in village D.
   a) How do you feel about tourists visiting your village?
   b) What might you gain from tourists?

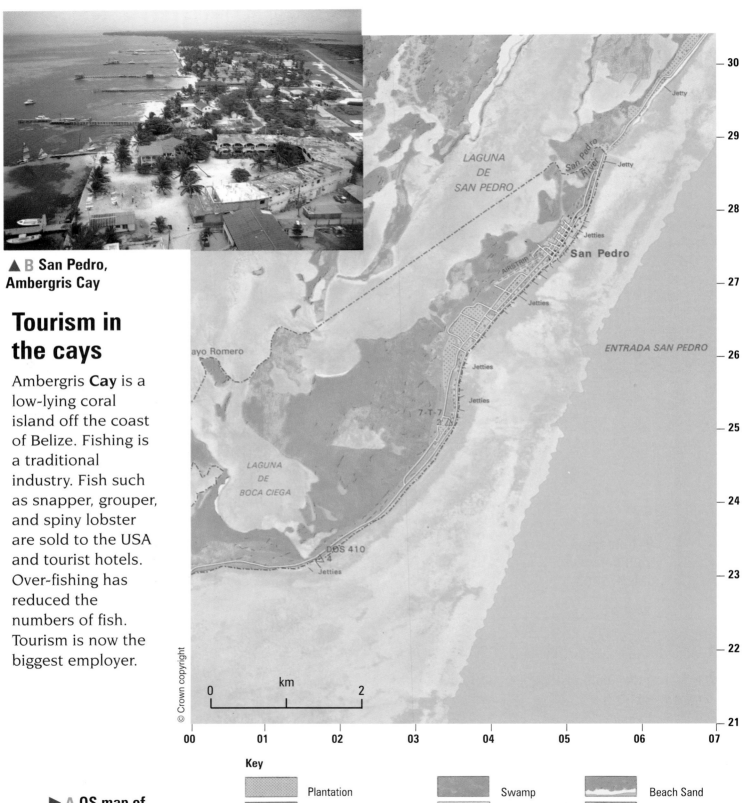

▲ B **San Pedro, Ambergris Cay**

Tourism in the cays

Ambergris **Cay** is a low-lying coral island off the coast of Belize. Fishing is a traditional industry. Fish such as snapper, grouper, and spiny lobster are sold to the USA and tourist hotels. Over-fishing has reduced the numbers of fish. Tourism is now the biggest employer.

© Crown copyright

km
0   2

► A **OS map of Ambergris Cay at a scale of 1:50 000**

Key

Plantation

Thicket and Mangrove

Mangrove

Swamp

Mud or Sand

Beach Sand

Coral or Tidal Flats

Hol Chan marine reserve

Hol Chan marine reserve is 6km south-west of San Pedro. It was set up in 1987. Fishing and diving are limited. Tourists pay a fee and can only visit some areas. Scientists keep watch on the reef and the fish. They compare the health of the coral and the number of fish with areas outside the reserve.

Fragile environments

Any environment can suffer from too many visitors. The number of people an environment can take before it is damaged is called its **carrying capacity**. A fragile environment has a smaller carrying capacity than a tough one. Coral is fragile – just touching it can kill it. Sewage from hotels causes algae to grow on the coral, which also kills it.

▲ **C Coral**

Up to 250 people visit the reserve each day. Some stand on the reef or break off coral. Then disease attacks the coral. The more tourists who visit, the more harm is done to the reef.

It would help if tourists were banned from some areas. Another way to solve the problem would be to make more reserves. The tourists would cover a larger area and do less damage in each place.

1 Use map A.
  a) Give a grid reference for San Pedro.
  b) Hol Chan marine reserve is 6km south-south west of San Pedro. Give its grid reference.

2 a) List the ways that tourism can damage the reef.
  b) Explain what is meant by carrying capacity.
  c) List the ways the reef can be protected from damage.

3 Give three reasons why tourism is important to Ambergris Cay.

4 What would happen if tourists were barred from visiting the reef? Discuss the advantages and disadvantages of this plan.

Tourism in the desert: Wadi Rum, Jordan

Jordan is a country in the Middle East. Tourists visit not only its deserts, but also its Red Sea coral reef and historic places. Wadi Rum is a small village in Jordan's desert. Tourists come on day trips from Petra or Aqaba. The village is often crowded with coaches and tourists. Photo A shows Wadi Rum.

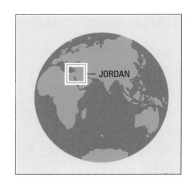

JORDAN

▼ **A Effects of tourism**

• Problems with sewage and litter
• Desert paths are eroded by jeeps
• Jobs and money for local people

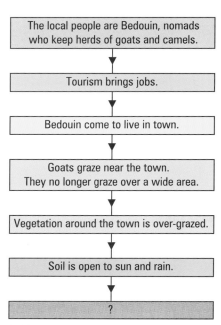

The local people are Bedouin, nomads who keep herds of goats and camels.

↓

Tourism brings jobs.

↓

Bedouin come to live in town.

↓

Goats graze near the town. They no longer graze over a wide area.

↓

Vegetation around the town is over-grazed.

↓

Soil is open to sun and rain.

↓

?

▲ **C Effects of tourism on the Bedouin nomads**

▼ **B Questions for tourists in Wadi Rum**

Why did you come to Jordan for a holiday?	%	How long will you stay in Wadi Rum?	No. of people
The desert scenery	37	Two hours	36
The weather	11	Six hours	77
Historical sites	34	One day	45
Biblical sites	8	Two days	29
Other	10	Longer	14

1 Use table B. Give the two main reasons why tourists visit Wadi Rum.

2 Use photo A. List the good and bad points of tourism in Wadi Rum.

3 Look at flow chart C.
   a) Write a label for the last box.
   b) How has life changed for the Bedouin? Give reasons for the changes.

Improving tourism in Wadi Rum

There are two plans for tourism in Wadi Rum. The first would encourage visitors to stay longer and spend more money. The environment would be protected. This plan includes:

- making desert paths and camping places for walkers
- building a visitor centre with information about the desert
- helping the Bedouin to stay in the desert with their animals
- building roads so that jeeps stay off the desert sands.

The second plan is to stop any growth in tourism.

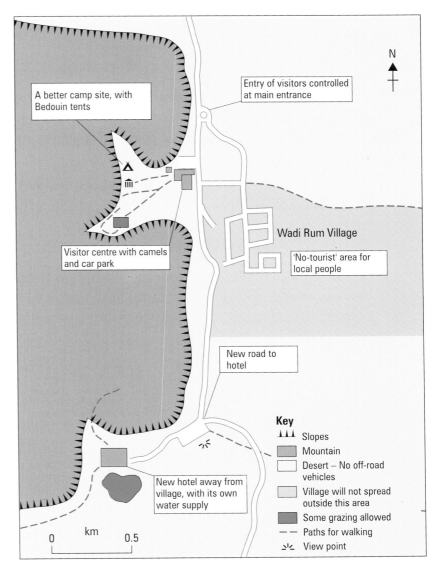

▲ **D** Ideas for tourist growth in Wadi Rum

4 Read about the plan shown in D. How will this plan affect:
a) local people
b) the environment?

5 In groups, make up your own ecotourism plan for Wadi Rum. Remember that ecotourism should do as little harm to the environment as possible and involve local people.

Review

- A growing tourist industry brings money to developing countries.
- The good effects of tourism need to be greater than the bad effects.
- A healthy environment is important for tourism.
- Ecotourism allows tourism to develop without damage to the environment.

Brazil

Brazil is a developing country in South America.

- **What is Brazil like?**
- **Brazil is rich in resources, so why do 50% of its people live in poverty?**
- **How can Brazil use its natural resources without damaging the environment?**

BRAZIL

A giant country

Brazil is huge. It is bigger than the European Union. It exports more iron **ore**, coffee, sugar cane, and oranges than any other country. Brazil has strong industries but many Brazilians are very poor.

1 Use map A.
a) With how many countries does Brazil share a border?
b) How long is Brazil's coastline? Think of a way to measure as accurately as possible.
c) Where are its largest cities found?
d) Name two tributaries of the Amazon river.

2 Use an atlas. Look at the size of Brazil compared to the UK. Write a sentence about Brazil's size.

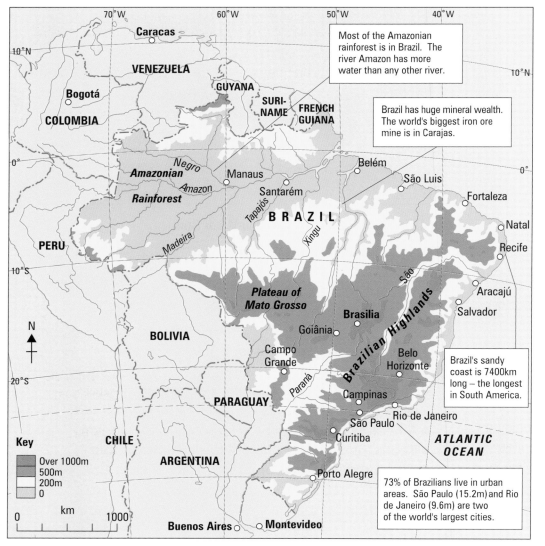

Most of the Amazonian rainforest is in Brazil. The river Amazon has more water than any other river.

Brazil has huge mineral wealth. The world's biggest iron ore mine is in Carajas.

Brazil's sandy coast is 7400km long – the longest in South America.

73% of Brazilians live in urban areas. São Paulo (15.2m) and Rio de Janeiro (9.6m) are two of the world's largest cities.

◄ A Brazil covers nearly half of South America (8.5 million km^2)

▲ B The city of Rio de Janeiro

▲ C Football on Copacabana beach, Rio de Janeiro. Brazil is the only country to have won the World Cup four times

Rich and poor in Brazil

There is great **inequality** in Brazil. This means that wealth is not spread out fairly between people. There are some very rich people but others are very poor indeed. Many rich and famous people live in Rio de Janeiro. Ayrton Senna, the Brazilian racing driver who died in 1994, lived there. But most people in Brazil do not share its wealth. About 30% of people in Rio de Janeiro and São Paulo live in *favelas*, or squatter settlements, built on land that they do not own. Another 25% live in poor housing. Worst of all, between 7 and 8 million children live on the city streets in Brazil.

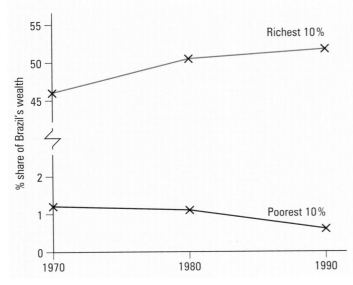

▲ D The widening gap between rich and poor in Brazil

3 Use map A and photo B. Make a list of the tourist attractions in Brazil.

4 Use graph D. Copy these sentences, choosing the right word.

In 1970 the *richest/poorest* 10% of Brazil's people owned 45% of its wealth. Since then the richest people have become even *poorer/richer*, while the poorest people have grown *richer/poorer*.

Child murder in Brazil

Brazil has between 7 and 8 million street children. Life for these children is very hard:
- 1064 homeless children were murdered in São Paulo from January 1991 to June 1992
- 277 homeless children were murdered in Rio de Janeiro between January and July 1992.

▲ A

◄ B

I'm Maria. I am 13 and I live in Rio. I left home because my stepfather beat me and my mum. Now the police beat me up. I'd like to go to school. Living on the streets is awful.

Law of the streets

Street children in Brazil sleep where they can, in underground stations, doorways, empty buildings, or on the beach. They hunt for food in rubbish bins or steal fruit from stalls. Some children steal to stay alive, mugging people for their watches, cameras, or money. Small children beg food from people in restaurants. Cold, hungry, and afraid, they keep together in groups. Some sniff glue.

Death squads often kill children, saying they are stopping crime and 'cleaning up' the city.

▲ C Adapted from *The Guardian*, 5 January 1993

Who is killing the children?

No one knows for sure. Many people think that local business people are paying for the children to be killed.

Crime and glue sniffing give the city a bad name.

Tourists won't come to Rio if beggars hassle them.

Street children do dirty work, like collecting litter, for very little pay. They need help, not punishment.

Don't blame the children. Their parents are too poor to look after them.

▲ D Opinions about the street children

	% of population	% who cannot read or write	Average income (US $ per month)
White	55.7	12.2	214
Mixed race	38.7	27.9	100
Black	5.1	30.0	87
Asian	0.5	7.4	377

▲ E Race and inequality in Brazil

Help for the street children

In 1992 an enquiry was held into the killings, but people were afraid to say what they knew. In May 1996, three policemen were tried for murdering street children and one admitted his guilt. Some people now help street children with meals, shelter, and finding work.

▲ F

90% were boys

80% were black

67% were aged 16–17

12% had appeared before a court

▲ **G Data on the murdered children**

Factfile: Tourism

- Tourism is important to Brazil.
- Tourism earned US $1 224 999 000 in 1992
- 80% of tourists stay one night or more in Rio.
- Many tourists are afraid of being robbed or mugged while in Rio.

1 a) List the problems facing street children.
b) List the problems street children cause the police.

2 Look at photos A and F.
a) Give a caption for each.
b) Imagine that you are one of the people in the photos. Write a description of your life in Brazil.

3 Discuss the opinions in D.
a) Do you agree with any of them?
b) Who do you think is to blame for the way street children have to live?

4 Make an information leaflet about Brazil. One side should show what attracts visitors (see pages 82–84). The other should show the side of Brazil that tourists do not usually see, such as child murders and poverty.

5 Look at G. Is it true that most homeless children are criminals ? Give your reasons.

6 Most street children are black or of mixed race. Using table E give one reason for this.

Inequality in Brazil's regions

We have seen examples of inequality in Brazil's cities. There is also inequality in the different regions of Brazil. Some parts of Brazil are rich, while other parts are very poor.

South-east Brazil

The south-east of Brazil is the richest part of Brazil. Its wealth comes from industry and **foreign investment**. This means that foreign companies put their money into developing firms in Brazil. 43% of the population live in the south-east. Industries in the south-east produce satellites, fighter aircraft, and cars. Off the coast an oil company is drilling for oil at great depths, as C shows.

▼ **A** The south-east region of Brazil

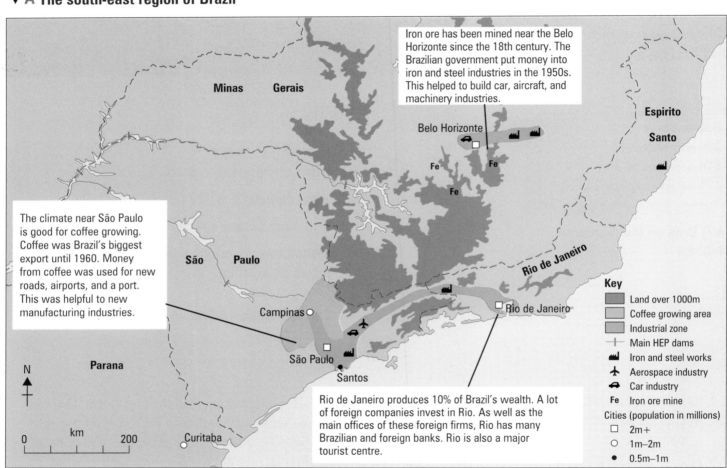

Iron ore has been mined near the Belo Horizonte since the 18th century. The Brazilian government put money into iron and steel industries in the 1950s. This helped to build car, aircraft, and machinery industries.

The climate near São Paulo is good for coffee growing. Coffee was Brazil's biggest export until 1960. Money from coffee was used for new roads, airports, and a port. This was helpful to new manufacturing industries.

Rio de Janeiro produces 10% of Brazil's wealth. A lot of foreign companies invest in Rio. As well as the main offices of these foreign firms, Rio has many Brazilian and foreign banks. Rio is also a major tourist centre.

Key
- Land over 1000m
- Coffee growing area
- Industrial zone
- Main HEP dams
- Iron and steel works
- Aerospace industry
- Car industry
- Fe Iron ore mine

Cities (population in millions)
- □ 2m+
- ○ 1m–2m
- ● 0.5m–1m

▼ **B** Regional differences in Brazil

Region	% population	% area	% of industrial jobs	Average income (US$)
North	7	42	3	3020
North-east	29	18	18	1890
South-east	43	11	57	3720
South	15	7	17	2960
Centre west	6	22	5	3290

1 Use map A.
  a) How has the coffee industry helped in Brazil's development?
  b) How has the steel industry helped in Brazil's development?

2 Name two ways in which Rio is important to Brazil.

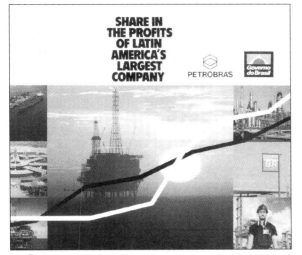

▲ **C** **A Brazilian oil company's advert**

How is the south-east changing?

São Paulo state is the most industrial state in the south-east.

- It is the size of the UK and has a population of 31m.
- It produces 37% of Brazil's wealth and 33% of its exports.

But now **manufacturing industries** are being replaced by **service industries**. It has become harder for factories to make a profit. Firms have to keep wages low and employ fewer people. For example, 900 000 cars were made in 1990 but in 1993, 1 400 000 cars were made with fewer workers. New firms in Minas Gerais and Parana have newer facilities, cheap land, less taxes, and weaker trade unions.

Skilled jobs have been lost in the factories. But the new jobs in service industries are often part-time and low-paid.

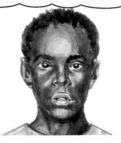

Factories in São Paulo have polluted the city. Three tonnes of chemicals and heavy metals go into the River Tiete every day. I'm glad factories here are closing down.

Strikes have lost firms a lot of money. The unions are making trouble.

São Paulo is overtaking Rio as a business and banking centre. Jobs in the service industries have risen from 50% in 1980 to 58% in 1993.

Unemployment went up to almost 15% in 1993.

▲ **D**

3 List the main industries in Brazil.

4 a) Describe the job changes in São Paulo's manufacturing industries.

   b) Describe the job changes in São Paulo's service industries.

   c) How has unemployment been affected by these changes?

5 Some people, as you can see in D, are pleased by the changes in São Paulo. Give the good points about the changes.

The north-east of Brazil

North-east Brazil is larger than all of the UK, France, Germany, and Spain put together. It has a population of 38 million. It is much poorer than the south-east, with less industry. Poverty, unemployment, and drought have meant that many people have been leaving this area.

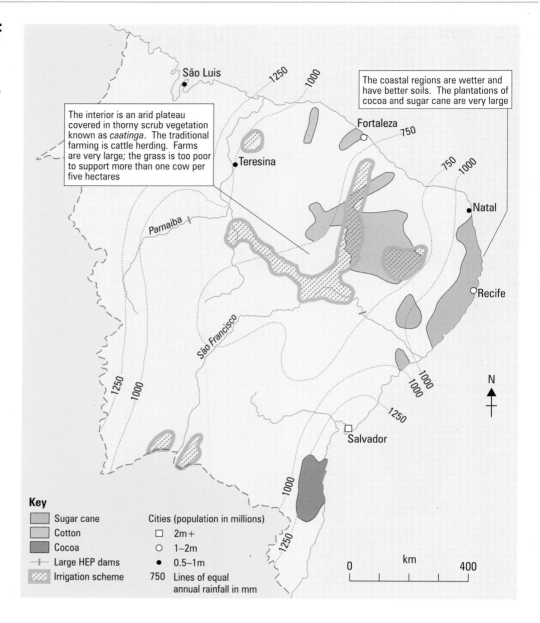

The interior is an arid plateau covered in thorny scrub vegetation known as *caatinga*. The traditional farming is cattle herding. Farms are very large; the grass is too poor to support more than one cow per five hectares

The coastal regions are wetter and have better soils. The plantations of cocoa and sugar cane are very large

Key

▨ Sugar cane		Cities (population in millions)	
▨ Cotton		▢ 2m+	
▨ Cocoa		○ 1–2m	
—┼— Large HEP dams		● 0.5–1m	
▩ Irrigation scheme		750 Lines of equal annual rainfall in mm	

km 0 — 400

▶ **A The north-east of Brazil**

1 Use map A.
  a) Give the population of:
     (i) Fortaleza (ii) Salvador.
  b) Give the rainfall in:
     (i) Fortaleza (ii) Salvador.

2 a) What is farmed in the driest areas? (Less than 750 mm of rain per year.)
  b) What has been built to solve the drought problem?

Rich and poor farmers

For 200 years the north-east of Brazil has been the world's biggest sugar producer. **Plantation** owners are very rich. Large plantations need few skilled workers, so there are many poor farmers who own no land. They are called **subsistence** farmers, which means that they grow just enough food to feed themselves. Expensive dams have been built which irrigate the large plantations. Smaller farmers complain that their land has been flooded. But the government has given them no help.

Moving from the north-east

Between 1970 and 1988, over 1.5 million people left the north-east – up to 60% of all Brazil's migrants come from this region. Small farmers from the north-east moved to the Amazon rainforest. The government gave them land, but no money or other help. The migrants burnt trees to make farmland, but their crops grew badly in the poor soil.

	GNP per person (US $)	Infant mortality (deaths per 1000 births)
Argentina	2780	29
Brazil	2920	57
North-east Brazil	1890	100
Costa Rica	1930	17
Cuba	1000	13

Drought hurts Brazil's poorest people

Francisco Alamedo can't remember when he last ate meat. He prays for rain. But it has not rained for three years. His land is dry. The beans he planted last year died. He earns $3 a week working on a plantation. His family live on meals of coffee, flour, and water. They go to bed hungry.

▲ B Adapted from *The Financial Times*, 12 March 1992

◄ C The north-east compared with the rest of Brazil and other Latin American countries

▼ D Migrants in 1990

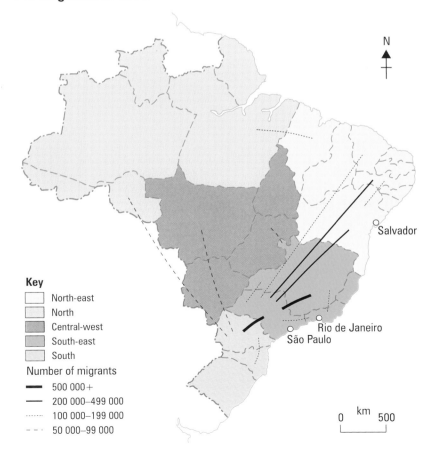

Key
- North-east
- North
- Central-west
- South-east
- South

Number of migrants
- 500 000+
- 200 000–499 000
- 100 000–199 000
- 50 000–99 000

3 Use map D. Where do most migrants in Brazil:
a) move from
b) move to?

4 Give their reasons for moving.

5 Use pages 86–88. Copy and complete this table to compare the two regions.

	South-east	North-east
People		
Farming		
Industry and jobs		

The Amazon rainforest

The Amazon River is huge and powerful. Its drainage basin is covered by the largest rainforest in the world. It contains few people, but huge amounts of wildlife – 10% of the world's plant and animal species are found there.

Using the Amazon

For thousands of years tribal people have used the forest without harming it. Map B shows how the Brazilian government have used the forest in the last 40 years.

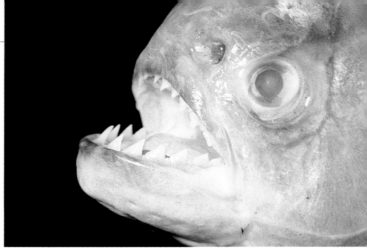

▲ **A** The piranha fish, from the Amazon river

Factfile: River Amazon

- The Amazon is 6640km long and is the second longest river in the world.
- 2000 different species of fish live in the river.
- The Amazon drains an area the size of Australia.
- The river carries sediment 200km out into the Atlantic.

▼ **B** How the Amazon rainforest is being developed

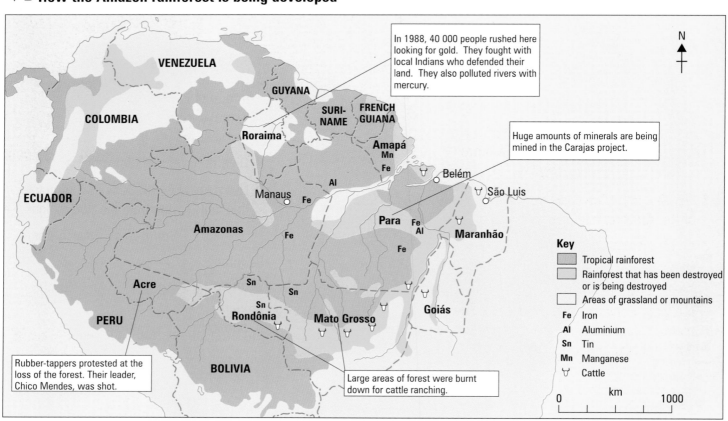

In 1988, 40 000 people rushed here looking for gold. They fought with local Indians who defended their land. They also polluted rivers with mercury.

Huge amounts of minerals are being mined in the Carajas project.

Rubber-tappers protested at the loss of the forest. Their leader, Chico Mendes, was shot.

Large areas of forest were burnt down for cattle ranching.

Key

▨	Tropical rainforest
▨	Rainforest that has been destroyed or is being destroyed
☐	Areas of grassland or mountains
Fe	Iron
Al	Aluminium
Sn	Tin
Mn	Manganese
⛨	Cattle

0   km   1000

The Grande Carajas Project

The Carajas region has huge deposits of iron ore, tin, gold, copper, and bauxite (aluminium). The European Union lent Brazil US $600 million in 1982. This helped Brazil to develop mining in the region. Huge areas of forest were destroyed to:

- build 900 km of railway from the mines to the port of São Luis
- provide charcoal for **smelting** ore
- build reservoirs and dams for hydro-electricity.

The Tucuri dam flooded 2160 km^2 of rainforest where 3600 Parakana Indians lived. Chemicals which were used to kill trees polluted the water and made the Indians ill.

▶ C **Part of the Carajas iron ore mine**

1 List the countries apart from Brazil where parts of the Amazon rainforest are found.

2 Copy and complete these sentences, filling in the gaps.

The Amazon rainforest is being destroyed. In the states of Rondônia and .... it has been cleared for .... In Para the forests have been cut down for .... in the .... project.

3 Where does the forest seem least in danger of destruction?

4 The development of the rainforest has upset local people. Give three different examples of this.

5 List the reasons why we should try to save the Amazon rainforest.

6 Make a poster to show the damage being done in Amazonia.

Conservation

The Brazilian government has listened to protests about the loss of its rainforest. It now tries **conservation** methods or ways to protect the rainforest and the wildlife that is left. Less than 2% of Brazil's Atlantic rainforest is left. Roads, farming, and industry have destroyed the rest. Some species of birds and monkeys may soon die out. In a conservation project, Jersey Zoo helps by breeding golden lion tamarins like the one in photo B. The tamarins are then set free in privately owned forest in Brazil.

Rights for people and animals

Brazil's new conservation laws protect the rainforest but they can make life difficult for local people. Many Indians live in protected areas so they cannot live as they used to do. But gold miners still destroy and pollute their land. Extract C shows that local people and conservationists can have different ideas about what is best for the forest.

▲ A The original Atlantic rainforest

▲ B This golden lion tamarin was born in Jersey Zoo, but will be sent to its rea home in Brazil's Atlantic rainforest

▼ C Adapted from *The Guardian*, 16 August 1991

Two million alligators live around Nhamunda, an Amazon town. The Brazilian government thinks that people are killing them to make money. Alligator skins sell for £60 each. They are used for shoes and bags. Brazil's government told local people to stop killing the alligators. But locals say they only kill alligators because they ruin their fishing nets. 'Alligators destroy 20 nets a month. We make our living from fishing.'

◄ D Alligator skins are valuable. But ecotourism is another way to earn money. This live alligator is being shown to tourists by a local Indian

1 a) Give one reason why tamarins are in danger of extinction.
b) What is being done to help tamarins?
c) How is the Brazilian government helping tamarins?
d) How is Jersey Zoo helping tamarins?

2 a) Name one way in which people can earn money from the Jacare alligator.

b) Why do local people wish to kill them?
c) Why does the Brazilian government protect these alligators?

3 Write a sentence to show the views of the following people about the Jacare alligator:
a) local fishermen
b) worker in the shoe and handbag industry
c) conservationist.

Review

- Brazil is a huge country.
- It has modern industries.
- There are huge inequalities between rich and poor.
- Brazil's cities have many poor, homeless people.
- Poverty has caused people to move from the north-east to Amazonia and the south-east.
- Much of the rainforest has been lost but people are making efforts to save what is left.

▼ E **How wealth is shared**

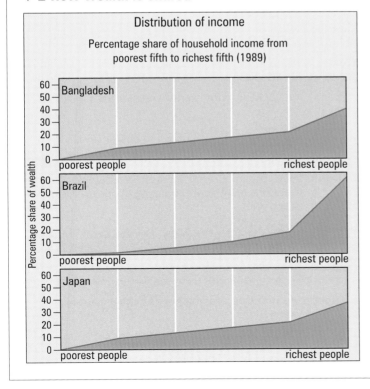

▲ F **Avon make-up is sold by 60 000 workers in Amazonia. The favourite face cream costs as much as two weeks' wages**

4 Use graph E.
a) Compare Brazil's poorest people with Japan's poorest people.
b) Compare Brazil's richest people with Japan's richest people.
c) Discuss the differences shown in Brazil's wealth compared with that in Japan and Bangladesh.

Glossary

Aerial view A view from the air.

Appropriate technology Simple tools or machines which can be mended easily and do not need expensive parts. They are useful in many developing areas.

Birth rate The number of babies born each year for every 1000 people.

Bunds Low earth walls built along the slopes of fields. They help to stop soil erosion.

Carrying capacity The number of people that an environment can hold without damage.

Cay The name given to a low-lying coral island.

Conservation Protecting the environment from the harmful effects of human activity.

Conurbation A large urban area formed when towns grow into each other.

Coral reefs Corals are tiny sea animals. They have a hard outer covering of limestone. They live together in vast numbers and form reefs.

Death rate The number of deaths in a year for every 1000 people.

Deforestation Cutting down trees and clearing forests. Land can be cleared for timber, farming, industry, or road building.

Dependants People who rely on other people for food, housing, or clothing.

Diversification Increasing the types of industry, crops, goods, or services.

Dykes Embankments which are built to stop flooding from a river or the sea.

Earth tremors The shaking of the Earth's crust made by an earthquake.

Economy The trade, industry, and money of a country.

Ecotourism Tourism which aims not to harm the environment.

Embankments Artificial river banks built to prevent flooding.

Epicentre The place on the ground that is right above the centre of an earthquake.

Exports Goods and services which are made in one country and sold to other countries.

Family planning Using birth control such as contraceptives to plan the number of children in a family.

Fault An area of weakness in the Earth's crust where volcanoes and earthquakes are likely to happen.

Favela A settlement built by people who live on land which does not belong to them.

Fire storm A super-heated wind which is pulled into the centre of a large fire.

Foreign investment When companies put money into factories or developments (such as a mine or dam) in a foreign country.

Fossil fuels Fuels made from the remains of dead plants and animals, buried in the ground (for example, oil, natural gas, coal).

Fuel reserves The amount of a fuel that is left to use.

Geothermal energy Heat from the Earth's crust. Cold water can be pumped into volcanic ground. Hot water that comes back can warm houses, or turn turbines.

Global warming The slow rise in world temperatures caused by the greenhouse effect.

Gorge A narrow steep-sided valley.

Greenhouse effect The warming of the Earth's atmosphere. Heat is trapped by 'greenhouse gases' such as carbon dioxide.

Groyne A low wall of concrete or wood built out into the sea.

Hydro-electric power (HEP) Electricity produced by the power of fast-moving water. Moving water is used to drive turbines which make electricity.

Inequality Where some groups of people have greater wealth or resources than others. There may also be inequality between countries or between regions.

Infant mortality The number of children in a year who die before their first birthday.

Informal work A job without a regular wage, such as selling goods on the street or recycling rubbish.

Irrigation Transporting water to dry areas, often for growing crops.

Landfill The tipping of rubbish onto the land.

Lava The name given to molten rock after it leaves a volcano.

Life expectancy The number of years the average person can expect to live. Diet, health care, housing, types of work all affect life expectancy.

Magma Molten rock under the surface of the Earth. When magma reaches the surface and flows out it is called lava.

Mangrove Trees which grow on tropical coasts, where fresh water from rivers mixes with salty sea water.

Manufacturing industry Making goods such as stereos, computers, televisions, and cars.

Mass tourism Where many people visit the same area. This often makes problems for the environment.

Migrant (migration) A person who moves from his or her home, often to look for work or food.

Natural resources Materials which are found naturally, such as timber, fossil fuels, and ore.

Non-renewable Non-renewable fuels can be used up – for example, the coal that we burn cannot be replaced. Renewable energy comes from sources which will not run out like wind and wave power.

Nuclear power Energy made in a nuclear reactor. Heat and electricity can be made using nuclear power.

Ore Rock from which useful minerals can be taken.

Peninsula A piece of land that is almost an island.

Pension Money paid by a company or the government to people who have retired from work.

Piece-rate Work paid by the number of pieces of work completed not by the hour.

Plantation A large area used to grow one type of crop such as tea, sugar, coffee.

Plates The Earth's crust is divided into jigsaw-like pieces which are called plates.

Population density The number of people per area of land.

Primary commodities Raw materials which have not been treated, like coffee beans, tea leaves, rubber, or tin.

Radiation The release of energy from radioactive materials such as uranium. High levels of radiation can cause sickness and death.

Rainforests Forests which grow near the Equator, where there is high rainfall and temperatures above 25°C. The largest rainforests are those in the Amazon Basin in South America and in Zaire, Africa.

Renewable energy Types of energy that are produced from sources that cannot be used up, such as wave and wind power.

Reservoir The artificial lake which forms when a river is dammed.

Salination When the amount of salt in the soil increases.

Sea defences Protecting land from the effects of waves and floods, for example, sea walls and groynes.

Semiconductors Microchips used in computers and high tech products.

Service industries Industries which are based on helping or serving people, for example serving customers in a shop or restaurant.

Silt Small pieces of sediment carried by a river.

Smelting Producing metal by melting the ore and taking out the impurities. This takes place at a smelter.

Soil erosion The movement of soil from an area by the wind or water. It often happens where the earth is bare and no plants are growing.

Street children Homeless children.

Subduction The downward movement of rocks and the Earth's crust at a place where two plates meet.

Subsistence When farmers produce only enough food to feed their families and not to sell to others.

Superdam Large dams over 150m high are known as superdams.

Transnational companies (TNCs) Companies with factories in several different countries.

Typhoon Violent storms which start over the sea in tropical regions. High winds, heavy rain, and large waves cause flooding in coastal areas.

Youthful population A population where a large percentage is under the age of 15.

Index